Self Mastery and Fate
With the Cycles of Life

H Spencer Lewis, FRC

The
Rosicrucian
Collection
®

Published by: The Rosicrucian Collection®
                       Greenwood Gate, Blackhill
                       Crowborough TN6 1XE
                       United Kingdom.

            Tel: +44-(0)1892-653197
            Fax: +44-(0)1892-667432
          Email: sales@amorc.org.uk

   UK Website: www.amorc.org.uk

International Website: www.amorc.org

Copyright: The Supreme Grand Lodge of AMORC, Inc.
                       © 1929, 1954, 1986, 1997, 2006, 2012
                       All Rights Reserved

ISBN-13:   978-0-9562753-5-6

Revised Edition © 2012
Printed and bound in the United Kingdom

DEDICATION

To the glory of
modern men and women

who are sufficiently broad in their
thinking to adopt new methods
to achieve success and happiness

this book is dedicated.

May it be a token of the first
step in their lives leading to

Self-Mastery

CONTENTS

The Law of Periodicity

There is a tide in the affairs of men
which taken at the flood leads on to fortune.

— Shakespeare —

To every thing there is a season,
and a time to every purpose under the heaven:
A time to be born, and a time to die;
a time to plant, and a time to pluck
up that which is planted.

— King Solomon —

FOREWORD

THE SYSTEM set out in this book is unique in several ways. First of all, it makes no pretence at being 'scientific' in any sense but is nevertheless based on a system which, though rigorous and clear in its assertions, and which has also been empirically tested many times over the decades since the book was written, has not yet been scientifically recognised or academically formalised.

Secondly, although it is not based on formal science, it is also not at the other end of the plausibility scale, namely, it is not based on weird and unfounded ideas that have no basis in reality. In fact as presented here it seems to be based on nothing more than careful observation. Don't be fooled though by its simplicity, for a comprehensive theory to back those observations certainly exists.

Thirdly, the *System of 7* as it is known, does not follow the pattern set out by Astrology, except indirectly; nor does it follow the system set out in the Tarot, the I-Ching, Palmistry or any other system of divination. It stands uniquely by itself and for those who understand its inner workings, it is one of the most important of all influences on the lives of people throughout the world.

And finally, whereas some divinatory systems, including

those just mentioned, have august histories and one can more or less gauge when and where they originated, the *System of 7* seems to have appeared from nowhere in the early 1920's. Publically at least, that is what it seems, though privately in esoteric organisations such as the Rosicrucian Order, the system has been the basis of a whole way of life for centuries.

Through this book, Dr Lewis revealed to the world in 1929 an ancient and until then secret system that very simply divides into seven periods of equal length, any activity or venture, any day, week or year, in fact any period that the human mind categorises as separate from all others. And to each of these periods, certain specific qualities are assigned that can have far-reaching consequences for our personal affairs and indeed the affairs of whole nations. Dr Lewis set out to describe in a simple, down-to-earth manner accessible to ordinary, non-academic people, the practical human interactions that occur as a result of the qualities associated with these periods, and in this regard he has certainly succeeded.

One may ask why just these specific qualities are assigned to the periods and not others. Why does the first period of any venture seem to be the antithesis of the seventh? Why does the third period in some mysterious way prefigure what happens during the fifth period of the same cycle? A deep and beautiful symmetry lies at the heart of the *System of 7* and can be used to benefit yourself, your family and friends in unique and beneficial ways.

Upon further investigation you will realise that the *System of 7* is not that unusual or unique. We see it operating all around us in nature, but especially so in the human mind and manner in which we have seemingly arbitrarily created our modern musical scale. For each octave, there are 12 semitones but only seven full tones, just as there are 12 astrological houses but only seven full houses in Dr Lewis' *System of 7*. Are the two related? They certainly are, but not because the two systems are related to each other, but that they both derive their existence from a far higher overarching set of universal principles.

Although Dr Lewis' main task is to give practical examples of what is favourable and what is not during each period discussed, he is, as any human would, making value judgements based upon his personal experiences in observing the *System of 7* in operation. This is unavoidable, so for your own sake, please realise that this book was written a long time ago in an era when moral values and even political and business norms were very different from our 21st century world-view. Despite this however, the material presented is so important and timeless that you would do well to consider it as though it were written yesterday. Human fashions change regularly, but human nature changes only very, very slowly.

The greatest favour you could do yourself, is to approach this book with a completely open mind and large doses of patience and tolerance until you have fully understood the system. As is the case with most people, you may have fixed ideas about what is and is not possible, what is and is not rational. Please put those ideas aside for now and try to absorb fully what Dr Lewis has to say.

Some things he says may astound you and may occasionally even offend. But be careful not to judge too harshly or too quickly. Instead, observe carefully your own life and how you have interacted with others during each of the 7 periods he describes. If you are ruthlessly honest and open with yourself in applying the criteria he gives, you will almost certainly be convinced before long that there is at the very least, a kernel of truth to this system..., and that is a good starting point, something worth pursuing!

The Editor
October 2012

Dr Lewis at the desk where he wrote many of his articles, short stories, books and lessons for Rosicrucian students.

1 The Problem of Mastership

W E ARE EITHER victims of fate or masters of our destiny! There are no two ways about it and no neutral positions. I am of course speaking of humanity in general and not of the individual, for there are individuals who are masters and creators of their destinies for part of their lives and innocent or despondent victims of fate at other times. The lives of such people prove that we can be masters or slaves as we choose.

The system set forth in this book for the attainment and application of self-mastership, or the mastership over so-called fatalistic conditions, is based upon the premise that *every human being is at least partially the creator of his or her environment and circumstances, and not merely the result of them.* Usually a premise is an assumption or supposition, though I trust that you will see before long that this premise is indeed based on solid facts and universal truths. All flows from this and it merely serves to verify and substantiate the solid foundation upon which the premise is based.

Therefore, if you are one of the many who believe that blind circumstance and the environment alone are what make or break civilisations and individual lives, controlling every aspect of them, I implore you for your own sake and in your own best interests to lay aside this belief while reading this book and testing its principles. At least for the duration of this book, keep an open mind and accept the premise upon which the system is based, thereby giving it every opportunity of serving you.

The fundamental principle involved in this system of self-mastery was observed centuries ago by untutored minds which had to depend upon the casual and multifarious manifestations of human existence and the operation of nature to determine natural laws in both the material and "spiritual" kingdoms. That principle, evolved through observation and perfected through test and application, reveals that all life, indeed all existence within the universe, has its expression in cycles, the periodicity of which is equivalent to the rhythm of certain measured and harmonious recurrences of stresses or impulses of a universal nature.

In its examination of the microscopic manifestations

of natural law, science has discovered that all living cells and in fact even crystals and other non-living matter have varying periods of rhythmic motion. These periods begin at "birth" and control the process of development to maturity, guiding the evolutionary steps preceding the process of breaking down or reproducing others of their own species. It has also been found that the periodicities that distinguish the rhythms within each of these species or classifications of matter are harmoniously related to the periodicities observable in the movements of the planets, the ebb and flow of the tides and the growth and decay of plant and animal life.

Even in the functioning of the organs of animal bodies, such as the breathing processes, the heart action and similar movements contributing to the maintenance of life, there is a definite rhythm closely resembling and having a harmonic relation to some of the larger and more pronounced rhythms of the universe.

I have no intention of being technical or academic in my explanation of the laws and principles pertaining to the cause of the universal rhythms governing the motion of life. Details of this are contained in the Rosicrucian teachings that are available to those who are devoting their lives to the profound research work in which Rosicrucians have been eminent for centuries. Suffice it to say that there are certain self-evident facts which supply the basis for further study in this direction.

In this book, I will specifically be referring to rhythms of life that affect us and our interests. Even a casual study of the system will open the doorway to such mastership of the practical affairs of our daily lives. There will be no room left in the minds of any who test the system, for uncertainty as to the universality of the laws involved. Their effect upon life and even things which seemingly are without life, will be adequately covered.

The question has often been discussed as to whether or not we really are free agents, in other words, whether or not we have free will. A test of the system contained in this book will reveal to you that, in so far as having the right and privilege to choose is concerned, you are indeed a free agent, absolutely and without doubt. But, you will also discover that not a personal God but an impersonal universal law holds you responsible for each and every choice you make, and forces you to accept the consequences of your choices.

Throughout our lives, we see the success of men and women who seem to have been fortunate in their choices of professions, occupations or applications of time; or who were "lucky" in their selection of property, material, place or time for the attainment of prosperity and happiness; or who regularly followed intuitive urges which actuated them in their affairs at most propitious times. But we also see those who seem to be unfortunate in all of these things, and in ignorance of the laws involved, we may be apt to attribute the fortunes and misfortunes of others and ourselves to "chance" or "fate."

It is the purpose of the system presented in this book to enable you to take advantage of, and work in harmony with, certain natural laws. The purpose is for you to master your fate, and through harmonious co-operation with the cycles of life, to reap the richest rewards offered by the bountiful disposition of what mystics of all ages have referred to as a "cosmic plan."

Without resorting to superstitious beliefs or practices, without invoking the questionable influence of hypothetical powers of an invisible nature, and with all the saneness and rationalism of a scientific method of living, practical men and women, even those who may be prejudiced against the so-called "metaphysical," may bring about important changes in their lives simply by applying the principles contained in this book.

With such a desire in mind, I urge you to carefully analyse with an open mind the brief explanations of the laws and principles that now follow. Neither slight them nor minimise their importance merely because of their simplicity.

2 The Free Agent

———————————————

IN CONSIDERING human actions as either free and controllable or as pre-destined, the important point to be examined is this: are our acts the result of prior causes, or are we directed in our affairs by external influences such as so-called "cosmic vibrations," mental impulses from without, or tendencies in and around us? In other words, are our lives and the way we live them merely an effect of the environment and various invisible impulses and urges over which we have no control? Or can we say that when certain opportunities or temptations are brought before us, we have a full and free will to either accept and utilise them or to deny and cast them aside?

Those who argue that the human being is a completely

free agent at all times, ungoverned by any external influences, are begging the above questions but reaching no conclusions. We are all fundamentally free agents in every sense of the word. Within reasonable bounds, we are free to do as we please precisely to the extent to which we are willing to live with the consequences of our choices. We can choose, select, elect and determine whatever we wish to do in each and every circumstance, and this implies that at the deepest levels of our beings, we can never be forced against our will to do or think anything we inherently disapprove of.

Of course, the real intent of the doctrine of free agency as promulgated by many schools of philosophical thought is to decry the fact that we are affected in any way by the "will of God," the autocracy of natural and "spiritual" law and the inevitable workings of heredity. Fortunately, these things do not however affect us in the sense usually presented by these philosophical schools, or by those who misunderstand the real principles involved.

The so-called "will of God" may be viewed as the operation of some overriding universal law, or as the dictates of an omnipotent, supreme being referred to by religions the world over as "God." We can choose whichever to believe in, or even reject the whole notion of a universal God, Law or Mind altogether. What cannot be disputed however, is that everything in the universe, humans included, are affected by some over-arching "law of everything," or in religious terms, the "supreme will" of a sole God. The method whereby this law or will of God is expressed and brought to our conscious awareness, is poorly understood even by those who have devoted their lives to a serious analysis of these laws and how they direct the operation of the universe.

The belief in a personal God who has destined and decreed for each of us, before birth, a course and career which will unfold regardless of our personal efforts to do otherwise, and regardless of the application of the divine power within us, is simply an erroneous belief. It is unsupported by the testimonies of life itself and by the revelations of certain natural laws when applied with insight and true understanding.

Through the present system, we can learn that the will of God, or this overarching universal "law of laws," is expressed to us in the form of intuitional inspirations expressed as inner tendencies, impulses or urges, or propitious presentations in the form of opportunities and temptations. And we are as often tempted to do good as to do evil. The same may be said of any of the true principles of planetary or other external cosmic influences. In each case, their effect upon us is in the form of these tendencies without the power to enforce their acceptance by us. Therefore, we find that we are constantly affected by opportune temptations to act or think in specific ways.

Merciful and just is God, the intelligent law that governs all that is, in giving us the power and privilege to make our own choices when we are presented with opportunities, urged by inspirations or led by impulses. And as free agents able to choose between one impulse and another, one inspiration and another, or one temptation and another, we must abide by our decisions and assume responsibility for their consequences.

Agreeing therefore that we are free agents and have the privilege and power to choose all our thoughts and acts, we still have to consider the nature and source of these impulses, urges and inspirations that come before us, demanding we make a choice. If there were no diverse opportunities presenting themselves and if there were no varying impulses, urges and inspirations occurring momentarily, hourly and daily throughout life, there would be no reason for us to have the ability and freedom to choose. We would then surely not have been given the ability to reason, think independently and to use our will power?

The unconscious machinery of a factory has neither the ability to analyse nor the power to act as a free agent. Of all living creatures, we are unique in possessing free will to such a high degree. And it may be no tribute to humanity in general to say that the majority makes its choices most often unwisely, and that only to the minority has been left the duty of advancing the species through the proper exercise of its great prerogative.

In 1918 I wrote a discourse on this subject and stated that impulses, inspirations and tendencies were continuously presented to us for our choice. *"In conjunction with the study of the law of compensation, this subject is worthy of a complete book which I may prepare if I find a demand for it.*" I believe the time has come for people in the western world to know more about these laws and to live in harmony with them as have the Masters of the East and the highly developed and successful people of the Orient.

People in business are constantly confronted in their daily affairs with the necessity of deciding between two plans, two urges, two propositions, two temptations, two "hunches." Or there may be several distinctly different impulses and plans before them calling for a choice. They are also confronted with the diverse tendencies of their affairs to choose between a greater development of some of them, or a curtailment of others. They are confronted yearly with the problem of expansion or contraction of their business interests. They find themselves face to face with important decisions that must be made, decisions that affect the present and future standing of their businesses and the success of their personal or business careers.

The woman in the home finds herself facing similar problems. From day to day there are often two urges, impulses and temptations presented by the affairs of the members of her family, the arguments of canvassers and sales persons, the perplexities of her husband's personal affairs which bear upon the growth and development of the family and its best interests, and her own personal and intimate affairs. Young men and women just starting their careers in business, or trying to establish themselves in a selected field of effort, find themselves continuously called upon in the quiet of their personal examinations to make decisions that will unquestionably affect the remainder of their lives. To them, as to all others, come the urges and impulses, the opportunities and temptations, the desires and wishes, with both negative and positive phases to be considered and a choice to be made.

As these people make their decisions, they determine their fates and establish their destinies. The fate of a day, like the fate of a year, may leave its fortunate or unfortunate results to affect the entire remaining life and career of a person or business. Yielding to an urge or an inspiration, or submitting to an impulse or temptation, or taking advantage of an opportunity with no other warrant or reason than the judgement based upon analytical reasoning, is equivalent in most cases to choosing between right and wrong by the toss of a coin. Our reasoning cannot rise higher than the premises upon which it is based. And those premises will be faulty if they do not include a knowledge of the external influences and natural laws governing our life and affairs.

As the system in this book will show, there is a periodicity or cycle of periods regulating unfortunate episodes in the life of each being. It also regulates the movement, progression, development and maturity of each thing in life that begins at a point and proceeds onward to a conclusion. This occurs whether that thing is a business proposition, a journey, the building of a house or factory, the buying and selling of merchandise, diseases and illnesses of the flesh, the conception and development of an embryo, movement of the tides, or anything that is created and brought into existence by natural laws through divine decree or personal volition.

By working in harmony with the periods of our own personal life and the periods of the business plan, proposition or creation of our thinking, the utmost success will be attained. Working in ignorance of them however, will bring frustration, failure, loss and defeat.

We are free agents and must choose whether or not we will work in harmony with the universal law of rhythm. Rightly or wrongly, we have to make a choice. But the result of our choice automatically follows and this inevitable result constitutes a manifestation of the law of compensation. If you choose correctly and work in harmony with this law, you will master your fate. But if you fail to choose correctly and work out of harmony with the law, you will become a slave to fate and the victim of a destiny unconsciously created.

3 Cosmic Rhythm and the Cycles of Life

FOOLISH PEOPLE ignore the phenomenal facts of life simply because they cannot understand the logical theory which explains them. With the power of logic, we can reason from the domain of possibilities everything that can be called a theoretical explanation of the cosmic rhythm that produces the various cycles of life. But with the same logic and reasonableness, we cannot negate the facts that have been observed.

One may claim that electricity does not exist because its source and nature are not known to us. Yet, it is clearly there, and through its manifestations it proves to be a fact in the phenomenal world. So we may ignore the invisible vibrations of cosmic rhythm and smile at the possibility of these things being divided into manifest cycles or periods, yet the phenomenal facts are quite observable and undeniable.

There is a body of knowledge revealing certain laws and principles of cosmic vibrations that science would label as being *hypothetical* but that mystics over the ages have always known to be *true*. A detailed explanation of these laws cannot be covered in this book as they deal with the fundamentals of the Rosicrucian teachings which are available only to members of the Rosicrucian Order, AMORC. Moreover, these principles would serve no purpose at this time, and as I believe that this book will be perused by those of the practical type of mind who seek a system that is workable and not requiring deep study, I will avoid any unnecessary postulations regarding universal laws of a cosmic or spiritual nature.

It is sufficient to say that all energy in the universe, of whatever nature, has but a single source, though its emanations and radiations are divided into various phases of undulations that Rosicrucians call *vibrations*. These undulations have certain periodicities or periods of kinetic and static manifestations, much like the radiations from the antenna of a transmitting radio station. We may think of these undulations as being of different wavelengths, different rates of vibrations, or different periods as we please; but the fact remains that the resulting effects from the different waves or radiations account for all forms of known and unknown energies in the universe.

I am going to presume that those interested in the study of vibrations realise that vibrations may be divided into a great many octaves of manifestation and that each octave may be divided into many distinct forms of being in both the spiritual and material worlds. Even the few octaves that cover the manifestation of sound give a wide variety of manifestations. Some of the rates within the octaves of sound may be so low as to be inaudible to the average person and manifest only through touch, while others may be so high as to be inaudible but manifest in light or other mental or metaphysical ways. Ordinary electricity is unquestionably another form of the periodic range of the universal vibrations, as is the divine essence of the soul, the vital life force of the animal body and the lower vibrations of vitality in plant and mineral life.

In addition to the above manifestations caused by the varying rates of vibrations of cosmic energy, we find that the energy controls and directs the rhythmic motion of all things in the universe. I hardly need remind you that motion is the fundamental principle of all material things and that if motion were eliminated in the universe, we would see, hear, feel and sense nothing. Matter itself is a result of the motion and vibration of subatomic particles, which causes atoms and molecules to manifest and produce the corporeal world we know. This motion and vibration comes from the motion and vibration of the rhythmic pulsations of cosmic energy.

Everything in the universe exists and manifests

according to a rhythmic cycle distinctly its own, and everything that has had a beginning or a start, whereby it became a distinct entity, moves forward in time in accordance with a cycle of progression distinctly its own. Those who have had the pleasure of reading Einstein's theory of relativity, coupled with other recent, simple explanations of the theoretical relationship of time, motion and space, will realise that time itself is an artificial relationship between motion and our consciousness and apprehension.

When it was learned that our sight-consciousness requires a minimum of $1/8$ of a second to apprehend an impression, and that the impression registered upon the retina of the eye remained in the consciousness $1/16$ of a second after the sight impression had left the retina, it was found that by having the sight impression last $1/16$ of a second and the consciousness of it remain for $1/16$ of a second, we had an apprehensive period of $2/16$ of a second (i.e. $1/8$ of a second divided into two parts, being $1/16$ of actual physical impression and $1/16$ of retentive impression). This was a discovery of experimental psychology coupled with a metaphysical analysis of the time element in conscious apprehension.

From this analysis came the invention of the kinescope which later evolved into the present-day motion-picture camera and projector. However, it is from the fundamental fact that objective, worldly consciousness requires the element of time to apprehend and translate its impressions into understanding, that we have become accustomed to associate a definite period of endurance or progression to the existence of all things. And we unconsciously establish a scale or standard of measurement of time in which we become conscious, in a relative manner, of the existence of every thing in life.

Long before Einstein, it was known to Rosicrucians who taught principles closely related to relativity and the fundamentals of time and space, that the psychic consciousness of a person does not require the element of time in its apprehension, whereas the objective or worldly consciousness does. Therefore, in the dream state or in any psychic state, the progression of facts evolving in the consciousness does not require the element of time for apprehension. The progression or sequence of events is disassociated from the objective standard of measurement of time.

Therefore, in a dream or in a psychic state of awareness, events may occur and be apprehended by the consciousness in a fraction of a second, though when translated by the objective consciousness into a waking-state experience, they may require minutes to explain and are associated with a period of time spanning minutes to several hours. It is not uncommon for a dream that seemed to cover the relatively objective period of an hour or more, actually required a negligible fraction of time to occur in the psychic state. In fact there is no reason to believe that occurrences in the psychic state have any period of the time element in them at all for they do not seem to progress in relation to our objective consciousness of time.

In simpler words, we may say that all events and all things existing as events are associated by the objective consciousness with time, since they require time to be apprehended by our objective minds. We cannot be conscious in an analytical way of two things at the same time. When we try to be conscious or mindful of two things coincidentally, we can only be conscious of them intermittently by having each different impression follow in sequence, giving each its allotted fraction of a second for apprehension.

Therefore, a woman reading a book may walk along the street among many pedestrians. She may be successful in reading and understanding every word on the page, and at the same time avoid collision with others and make the proper progressive steps, side-steps and hesitations necessary to complete her walk. She may think that she is simultaneously conscious of her walking and reading, but in reality, she is rapidly dividing her attention between the words on the page and the steps she is taking. Such alternation in conscious apprehension or realisation may be so rapid as to seem almost coincidental. It is not the actual *progression* of events that requires the element of time; it is our *conscious awareness* of that progression that does, and this is always something relative, having no foundation in universal terms.

The observable progression of events is impressed upon the consciousness in such periods of time as constitute what is known as a *definite periodicity* or a *definite cycle*, and each and every event begins a cycle of its own through which it progresses to culmination or finality. These cycles are called the *rhythm of life* when associated with our own existence as human beings but more popularly are called *cycles of progression* when related to our material affairs.

Each human being has a cycle of existence that is divided into identical periods for all persons. The cycle begins with the first breath of life and lasts for approximately 144 years. Few, if any, have ever completed this cycle of life because of violation of natural laws or inharmonious living. Worldly events have two cycles, one called the *major* and the other the *minor*. The major cycle is one solar year, or approximately 365 days, while the minor cycle is one solar day, or approximately 24 hours. Other events or affairs in our lives such as ill-health in the form of diseases, accidents and fevers, also have cycles varying in length according to the nature of the thing itself, just as the gestation of human and animal embryos have cycles of distinctive lengths, and seeds in the ground have cycles of dormancy and germination.

Each cycle is divided into periods of equal length and each of these periods produces certain definite effects upon the progression of the thing governed by the cycle. What is meant by this will be explained in the next chapter, but here the important point to remember is that within our bodies, certain basic biological functions such as breathing, the beating of the heart and the functioning of other organs, follow particular rhythms in accordance with periodicities which are all well known. Any alteration of this rhythm plainly indicates to a physician that an abnormal condition exists.

So it is that all things in life move rhythmically, and the normal and natural rhythm for each thing in its cycle is in harmony with the overwhelming power and force of cosmic rhythms. When anything has a rhythm that is out of step with these cosmic rhythms, it is abnormal and therefore on its way to destruction. It is by being in rhythm with the cosmic or in tune with the infinite that we may keep our health and affairs progressing to the highest degree and manifesting abundantly in health, happiness, prosperity and peace.

4 The Periods of Earthly Cycles

IN THE PRECEDING chapter I said that as the human being is a physical entity, so is each event or each thing created by nature or humankind and having a definite, physical beginning, also an entity, having a cycle of existence distinctly its own. This refers even to diseases or to accidents, so-called, for they too result from our actions or inactions, and are therefore created by us, thereby defining a precise starting point and cycle of existence for each event.

Cycles of time for the existence of things can be thought of as lines drawn from starting points and continuing for various lengths. Each of these lines can be divided into periods as sections of equal length, and each of these sections can be viewed as a different manifestation of cosmic urges, impulses or influences, tending to direct the progress and development of each thing.

The philosophers of ancient Greece accepted the statement that in the beginning of creation, "God geometrised." The more we delve into the origin and operation of spiritual and natural law, the more we find that the whole scheme of the universe and the incidental scheme of each individual thing in the universe, operates and manifests in accordance with the principles of geometry. God therefore, can be considered as the Great Architect or the Great Mathematician, and the very complex map of geometrical motions and designs for the movement and existence of all things is only slowly being comprehended by us.

We may never know the origin and general plan of the entire universe and we may never know the reason for the mathematical progression of all events. But we can know through observations, tests and trials, the effects that these mathematical progressions have on our own lives.

I have stated that each event begins at a starting point, which is the beginning of a line of progression. This line constitutes a mathematical cycle equivalent to a sinusoidal curve beginning at the conception and birth of an event, attaining the peak of the curve at its maturity and declining along the curve to the last point of culmination or finality. The expression, "the course of events," is based upon a very ancient and continuous observation of the fact that most events reveal very clearly a definite course of progression. This fact has been considered so little in the business world by the busy materialist that he or she has overlooked one of the most helpful of all metaphysical principles. Rosicrucians however, constantly map their lives and daily affairs in accordance with specific mathematical cycles of operation throughout life. Hence the secret of their success and abilities to master their lives instead of being victims of so-called fate.

Rosicrucians begin their studies by carefully digesting the fundamental cycles of life, and acquaint themselves with the periodicity of as many things as possible. Eventually they become acquainted through these studies with their own relationship to the cosmic cycles and those periods wherein they may do the most desirable things at the most propitious times. It is this that has gained for some Rosicrucians through the centuries the title of Master, for they have become masters of their own lives and affairs.

We may liken the line that represents the progressive course of events in life to the charted line drawn upon a map that the captain of an ocean liner tries to follow when he leaves the port of New York expecting to reach the port of Liverpool. That line upon the map may be several thousand miles long, or it may be said to be seven days long. In the latter case, we may say that the cycle of the journey across the ocean, or the progression of the journey, is seven days long and is divided into seven periods of one day each. The first period of one day begins at the hour and minute the ship starts from the wharf. The second period of one day begins 24 hours after that and the other periods follow in the same manner. Hence, the journey is a cycle of seven periods and we would say therefore, that the periodicity of the cycle of the journey is seven days or seven periods.

Each of these days will produce a different effect in the events of the journey. The first day may produce or manifest a rough sea, with wind and storms. The second day may produce a calm sea, with every advantage for progressing rapidly and making up for time lost during the first day. The third day may produce not only a calm sea but also a warm climate, with a favourable wind enabling everyone to enjoy the journey to the utmost, and enabling the ship to make more rapid headway. The fourth day may produce a moderate sea but a strong headwind that will delay the journey; and the other days may produce still different effects. If the captain and passengers knew the true periodicity of their journey, they would be prepared for certain events and instead of being victims of fate, they would be forewarned and forearmed to be masters in every condition and circumstance.

The journey of life is much like a journey on the sea and each life begins at a slightly different starting point. Even casual observation revealed long ago that human life is divided into periods like the days of the ocean journey with definite events occurring during each period. The average person is unaware of these periods and still more unaware of any knowledge about the events that are most apt to occur during each of these periods. Therefore, he or she is unprepared to meet them until they are in full manifestation, and is handicapped in solving the problems of life by a lack of knowledge regarding the propitiousness of the tendencies which will be made manifest in each successive period.

The course of a business, whether it be manufacturing, selling merchandise, or some other line of endeavour, has a definite cycle or series of cycles of one year each, beginning with the first day that the business began to operate or the owner or proprietor entered into it. And each of these yearly periods or cycles is divided into segments of definite lengths wherein certain tendencies, conditions and circumstances are sure to arise or present themselves, and which may be most unfortunate if unknown or misunderstood, and exceedingly fortunate if appreciated and advantageously accepted.

So we see that the cycles of life really constitute a geometrical map or mathematical scheme whereby we can mechanically and accurately map our lives and the external influences on it, and either take advantage of these things or innocently and ignorantly submit to them. On the one hand we are masters of our destiny and on the other, we are victims of our fate.

5 The Simple Periods of Human Life

With Description of Cycle No. 1

O NE OF THE simplest and most apparent cycles of human life is one that the ancients observed and quickly learned to use as a basis for many of their mathematical and geometrical plans of life activities. Even in modern medicine and in many of the newer statistical forms of analysis of economics, this ancient cycle of human life is utilised as a fundamental scheme.

According to this primary cycle, human life is divided into a progression of periods, each period lasting approximately seven complete solar years or seven years of approximately 365 days each. Merely as an illustration of how this simple cycle manifests itself and not to use this cycle as a part of the system to be explained later on, I will call your attention to the fact that we can easily divide our lives into periods of seven years and notice how each period has brought its definite results or produced effects upon our growth, development and mastership.

Period No. 1 – Birth to 7th Year

Consider the first period of seven years. This is the time during which our babyhood and early youth occurs and when the fundamentals of our education and cultural development are formed. It is a period of self-discovery as far as the objective, material world and our relation to it are concerned. We learn to walk and talk, control our bodies and relate ourselves properly to our physical environment.

Period No. 2 – 7th to 14th Year

In the second period of seven years certain physical changes take place in our development and the mental side of our natures takes a secondary place in the changes going on. It is just before the fulfilment of the second period that the important physical changes in both boys and girls occur, preparing them for the third stage. If these changes do not occur before the end of the second period, the child is psychologically and physiologically behind and the sciences of physiology and psychology have both tacitly recognised this second period in the cycle of life.

Period No. 3 – 14th to 21st Year

In the third period of seven years, the physical and mental changes take secondary place, and it is primarily the psychic side of human nature that is developed. This brings about a greater sense of responsibility, giving dignity, poise and character to the individual. It is during this process that the individual attains that degree of psychic or psychological, as well as mental and physiological development, that establishes the individual as a capable entity qualified to assume legal responsibilities. The person who does not attain this degree by the 21st year is a late developer and is sometimes considered as incompetent or backward.

Period No. 4 – 21st to 28th Year

In the fourth period of seven years there is a development strongly centred in the emotional nature, carrying on the unfoldment of the emotional spark that was awakened in the preceding period. During these seven years, the individual acquires stability, a further sense of responsibility, a softening of the nature and a gradual activity in those higher, dormant faculties known as intuition, mental telepathy, unconscious psychometry and similar psychic faculties, together with an awakening interest in music, art, language and what may be termed the religious and higher things in life. An absence of any manifestation of the development of these faculties during this period would indicate to the psychologist or psychiatrist a subnormal development.

Period No. 5 – 28th to 35th Year

In the next period of seven years we find the creative processes of the mind most active and the ability to visualise, imagine and mentally create is greatly developed, with a developing attunement with the cosmic consciousness and the ethical standards of life. It is during this period that inventors have made their greatest progress and business men and women have become energetic and successful. It is also noteworthy that it is during this period that many of the world's greatest philosophers, avatars and mystics experienced a sudden cosmic Illumination that amounts to a complete attunement with the cosmic consciousness. The greatest of these began their worldwide missions and wrote their greatest works during this period.

Period No. 6 – 35th to 42nd Year

In the next period, men and women enter a stage of development that induces in them a desire to explore, investigate and reveal great knowledge and the hidden facts of life. A restlessness enters their nature, making them dissatisfied with the monotony of selfish and personal attainment and quickens in their beings the humanitarian emotion which makes them want to share what they have with the world. If they have little else than time and knowledge to share, they want to explore or discover and bring these revealed things to others for their benefit.

It is during this period that one starts disposing of the wealth one has accumulated or inherited, by building libraries or contributing to the arts, sciences, schools, colleges, universities, or explorative and inventive expeditions and speculations. It is truly the culminating period of all the years that have preceded in the life of the average human-being and starts the system of compensation in the average individual's life whereby the individual feels the need to return to the cosmic and to humanity some of the benefits he or she has enjoyed.

Period No. 7 – 42nd to 49th Year

In the next period the desire to rest, meditate and philosophically speculate builds up in the person a new chapter which unfolds strongly and uniquely in each case until he or she becomes a new person with new hopes, new desires, a new viewpoint in life and a new goal and ideal toward which to labour. The mind is turned more strongly toward religion and philosophy than to business and to those humanitarian activities that bring consolation and peace, by giving help, health and happiness to the downtrodden, disconsolate or despondent.

So surely does this period work out in the average person's life to some degree, that one may easily judge the approximate age of any eminent person by noting the tendencies of his habits and the trend of his thoughts, even when such a person is in very moderate circumstances and can do nothing more than wish he were able to do the things that he has in his mind and heart.

Period No. 8 – 49th to 56th Year

In the next period of seven years we find a tendency toward further retirement from personal or selfish ambitions, accompanied by a gradual lessening of the vitality and physical prowess but compensated for by a highly attuned psychic and mental nature. Here the pendulum is beginning to swing from the building up of a physical being to the building up of a spiritual being. For this reason, the physical body begins to lose its power to combat disease and to surmount the strains of accidents and undue strains upon the vitality. Statistics prepared by insurance companies plainly show the great changes in the physical body that take place during this period and the preceding one as the pendulum begins to swing from the physical to the spiritual.

Period No. 9 – 56th to 63rd Year

In the period of the next seven years there is a continuation of the conditions in the preceding period but accompanied now by a mellowing of the mental faculties together with a weakening of the physical prowess, leaving the individual more and more a psychic and spiritual being in harmony with the entire purpose of the cycle of progression. As we are born to become living souls and not merely soul-animated physical bodies, so we evolve, period by period, from birth to our 63rd year, from the physical being to a spiritual being, thereby approaching more closely the inevitable purpose of our existence.

The following periods of seven years each contribute to the spiritual development and gradual breaking down of the physical body. The end of the cycle is approximately at the 144th year, in order that the cycle of life may harmonise with other cycles and other periods that will be dealt with later.

So we can see in this very simple cycle of seven-year periods a rhythm of life that is universal for all and in accordance with a plan that is incomprehensible unless we study all of the cosmic laws and know, as Rosicrucians do in their higher teachings, the universal scheme of cosmic rhythm.

One question may be asked here: "If this is a universal cycle with all beings, will it manifest the same effects in the lives of those who live in primitive sections of the world as it does with those who live in the more modern and enlightened sections?" In answer to this, we can only say that observation has shown that the cycle manifests its effects in every human being in accordance with the individual's progress through the larger cycles of universal life. In other words, the manifestations in each individual's life are in accordance with his or her stage of evolutionary development.

Whether one believes in reincarnation or not, one cannot deny the effects of hereditary evolution, or the evolutionary effects of progressive generations. Each generation of human beings of a normal type is brought to a higher degree of susceptibility to the influence of these cycles of life. To primitive people in some parts of the world, the various periods outlined above would bring only such manifestations and changes in their nature as would be in keeping with their stage of evolution, or in other words, in keeping with their degree of progress along the higher cycles of universal life. To a lesser degree, there is considerable variation in these manifestations among those who are of one nation, culture or race in even the most enlightened parts of the world.

We may compare these seven-year periods of the cycle to the individual notes of an octave on a piano. Each octave has its notes separated into definite periods or rates of vibrations, and the periods in one octave are identical with the periods in another octave. We may say then that primitive people are living through cycles of life that are comparable to one of the lower octaves on the piano keyboard and although they pass through the periodic notes of that cycle, they do not manifest through themselves the same attunement or tone with harmonic vibrations that people elsewhere in the world would manifest who might be passing through one of the higher octaves.

According to the principles of reincarnation and the

evolution of character and personality, each human being passes through successive cycles like progressing through the various octaves of the keyboard from the lowest to the highest. We have no conscious awareness of what the lowest and higher octaves of the cycles of life are, for life itself is continuous and immortal and consequently can have neither a beginning nor an ending.

6 The Yearly Cycle of Human Life

With Description of Cycle No. 2

IN THE PREVIOUS chapter, I outlined the life cycle of each human being covering approximately 144 years and divided into periods of seven years each. Now we have another cycle to deal with, which will be referred to in the system explained later in the book as Cycle Two. This cycle has to do with our annual personal worldly affairs.

Cycle two is one calendar year of approximately 365 days in length. It renews itself and starts over again at each one of our birthday anniversaries. Therefore, the duration of cycle two is from birthday to birthday. The cycle is divided into seven periods of approximately 52 days each. This means that each year of our lives, from birthday to birthday, is divided into seven periods during each of which certain conditions are favourable or unfavourable for the things we wish and must do in the course of our earthly existence.

Although this cycle can on a first reading appear to be somewhat complex, if you carefully follow the tables, illustrations and explanations given in this chapter, you will have no trouble in understanding and utilising cycle two to aid yourself in attaining self-mastery.

As stated above, cycle two runs from birthday to birthday. It has nothing to do with the western calendar beginning on 1st January and ending on 31st December. This means that each individual has his or her own personal annual cycle. The only way in which two or more people may have the same cycle would be if they were born on the same day.

If you were born for instance on 20th March, then your yearly cycle is from 20th March to the following 19th March, each year of your life. With a person born on 2nd June, the cycle would run from 2nd June to the following 1st June. This point must be kept in mind to avoid confusion with the calendar year that runs from 1st January to 31st December. Remember also that this cycle has nothing to do with the astrological periods that begin and end around the 21st to 23rd of each month.

Therefore, in working out the seven periods of each

of your yearly cycles, you must begin by dividing your year into sections of approximately 52 days each. If you were born for instance on 20th March, you would begin with that day and count forward 52 days and then another 52 and another 52 and so on. Do the same if you were born on 2nd June, or on any other day.

For your convenience in calculating these periods, I have included a 365 day calendar in Chart A. This calendar is sufficiently accurate in its number of days to use for any year, regardless of whether the year is a leap year or not. You will note that the days of the months run consecutively after the name of each month. This makes it a simple matter to work out the 52-day periods of your personal life cycle, namely, cycle two.

Let us take an illustration now of a person born on 25th November which happens to be my birthday. My yearly cycle begins on the 25th of each November and ends on the 24th. We will start therefore with the calendar and write on a piece of paper the date 25th November, and begin working out the first period of 52 days by counting on the lines of the calendar 52 days forward from 25th November.

First we count 5 days to the end of November and then begin with 1st December as the 6th day and go on through December. The end of December gives us 36 days, so we continue counting in January and find that the 52nd day falls on 16th January.

Chart A - Calendar For Any Year

January	1	2	3	4	5	6	7	8	9	10	11	12	13	14	15	16	17	18	19	20	21	22	23	24	25	26	27	28	29	30	31
February*	1	2	3	4	5	6	7	8	9	10	11	12	13	14	15	16	17	18	19	20	21	22	23	24	25	26	27	28	29		
March	1	2	3	4	5	6	7	8	9	10	11	12	13	14	15	16	17	18	19	20	21	22	23	24	25	26	27	28	29	30	31
April	1	2	3	4	5	6	7	8	9	10	11	12	13	14	15	16	17	18	19	20	21	22	23	24	25	26	27	28	29	30	
May	1	2	3	4	5	6	7	8	9	10	11	12	13	14	15	16	17	18	19	20	21	22	23	24	25	26	27	28	29	30	31
June	1	2	3	4	5	6	7	8	9	10	11	12	13	14	15	16	17	18	19	20	21	22	23	24	25	26	27	28	29	30	
July	1	2	3	4	5	6	7	8	9	10	11	12	13	14	15	16	17	18	19	20	21	22	23	24	25	26	27	28	29	30	31
August	1	2	3	4	5	6	7	8	9	10	11	12	13	14	15	16	17	18	19	20	21	22	23	24	25	26	27	28	29	30	31
September	1	2	3	4	5	6	7	8	9	10	11	12	13	14	15	16	17	18	19	20	21	22	23	24	25	26	27	28	29	30	
October	1	2	3	4	5	6	7	8	9	10	11	12	13	14	15	16	17	18	19	20	21	22	23	24	25	26	27	28	29	30	31
November	1	2	3	4	5	6	7	8	9	10	11	12	13	14	15	16	17	18	19	20	21	22	23	24	25	26	27	28	29	30	
December	1	2	3	4	5	6	7	8	9	10	11	12	13	14	15	16	17	18	19	20	21	22	23	24	25	26	27	28	29	30	31

*In Leap Years there are 29 days in February.

CHART B
Example of Cycle No. 2 or No. 3
Starting on 25th November

Period No: 1	25 November	to	16 January
Period No: 2	17 January	to	8 March
Period No: 3	9 March	to	30 April
Period No: 4	1 May	to	21 June
Period No: 5	22 June	to	12 August
Period No: 6	13 August	to	3 October
Period No: 7	4 October	to	24 November

Therefore, we write on our piece of paper opposite 25th November the date 16th January and then opposite this, Period 1. This means that for a person born on 25th November, the first period of his or her yearly cycle is from 25th November to 16th January.

To find the second period of 52 days we start again at 16th January and count forward through January and February and partly into March until we have counted off 52 more days, which brings us to 8th March. So we write on the paper again under the first line, the two dates, 17th January to 8th March and right opposite this, Period 2.

Again we begin with 8th March and count forward 52 days, which brings us to 30th April. We write down the dates again, 9th March to 30th April and put opposite it, Period 3. Continuing in this way we find that the fourth period is from 1st May to 21st June; the fifth period is from 22nd June to 12th August; the sixth period is from 13th August to 3rd October; and the seventh period is from 4th October to 24th November.

These dates are approximate because we are laying aside the few hours that should be added each day to make the exact period of 52 days, 3 hours and 24 minutes. If any of the periods are minus or plus one day, it will not make much difference in the application of the system. If your last period of 52 days falls a day ahead of your birthday, this will make little difference in the use of the system.

With a person born on 8th February, the first period would be from the 8th February to 1st April, by counting 52 days from 8th February. And the second period would end on the 23rd May by counting 52 days from 1st April. To work out these periods in your life is not a difficult matter; simply use the calendar to count off the days. The important thing to bear in mind is to write on a piece of paper the seven periods of your year and to number these periods from one to seven. These you should call your cycle 2 periods. I am going to give you a third cycle shortly that is also very important and is divided into the same seven periods. Those periods will be called the cycle 3 periods and should not be confused with the cycle 2 periods outlined in this chapter or the cycle 1 periods outlined in chapter five.

Each period in cycle 2 contains opportunities, conditions, urges, influences, temptations and cosmic effects which have an important and subtle bearing upon the success or failure, strength or weakness, joy or sorrow, of your personal affairs, and I will now outline these things.

Period No. 1

During the first period of 52 days, you should use all your personal powers and abilities to advance your interests among people of influence who have powers or privileges to grant or to give. It is a period when solicitation should be made for favours, either in seeking employment, benefits, loans, partnerships, investments, special concessions, releases or even favours in the form of time, or postponements or dismissals in court.

It is an especially good period to seek favours or honours, help or recognition, from people who are in high power or high positions such as government officials, judges, mayors, governors, senators, people at the heads of large corporations or big businesses, or people who hold valuable papers, documents and matters that may be of great importance and which may be released, modified or otherwise affected by your solicitation.

This is also a good period for advancing oneself among the populace, or with the people of your city, state or country, or in building up your credit standing or your reputation with newspapers and influential people. It is a time to push yourself forward with discrimination and yet determination, for all of the cosmic vibrations are in favour of boosting and helping you personally so far as your name, reputation, honour and integrity among high persons or the public are concerned.

Period No. 2

Period 2 is distinctly different from period 1, for during these 52 days everything will tend to be favourably directed toward your plans regarding any journeys, especially those that are not for durations of many months or years, but are short and of immediate importance rather than of importance in the future. Journeys by water or by train are generally favoured during this period. It is also an excellent time for moving one's home to a new location, moving one's business or changing one's occupation if it is something under one's own control. In other words, this is a period for changes which are quick and soon over with.

In a business way this period will be found very favourable for such activities as pertain to movable things and things of indefinite location. Moving freight or dealing with freight business, express, cars, wagons, carriages, trucks, public vehicles, public lectures, shows, performances and things of this nature will be successful. Strange to say, this period is also an excellent one for those who are dealing with liquids, chemicals, milk, water, water power, petroleum, or other things of a liquid nature. Dealing with people who are in lines of business associated with all of the previous will also be more successful in this period than in any other.

Conversely, one should not plan a change of business, start a new career in business, or attempt to build anything permanent upon any change that is made during this period. Moving your home may be successful if done during this period, whereas buying a new home during this period may result in a future change, because changes made during this particular period do not make for permanency. Therefore, all things done during this time should be of such a nature as to begin during the period and end shortly afterward, or to be of the present months or year rather than the future.

This period is also good for people who are in businesses such as catering to the homeless or to fluctuating business affairs, such as those who operate hotels, direct traffic or cater to people who are constantly moving or passing by. It is also a good period in which to engage new employees, or to begin any agricultural developments or planting. Contracts, agreements, legal papers and other business affairs that are intended to continue over a period of years or remain permanent matters, should not be started or completed during this period.

It is an unfavourable period in which to borrow or lend money and is not good for the construction of any building or the starting of any business that requires considerable investment meant to last over a long period. Certainly, it is an unfavourable period to speculate in the stock market or to gamble in any form.

Period No. 3

Here we have a period that may be fortunate or unfortunate according to the application of the Cosmic powers and the discretion and discrimination that a person uses. This period fills the individual with an almost uncontrollable impulse to want to do great and important things and the fiery energy that goes through the human system during this period wants to express itself in many ways. If directed carefully, period 3 can be one of the greatest in the whole year for the building up of a business and the accomplishment of those things that call for great physical energy, physical effort, endurance, vitality, determination and persistency.

On the other hand, if the energy is misspent, or applied without discrimination and judgement, great tasks may be undertaken or started that will not be completed in a long time, and too much for one person may be started through the restless energy that wants to express itself. This is an excellent period in which to overcome those obstacles and conditions that in past periods seemed to check every advancement because of the energy and labour required.

It is an excellent period to begin anything that has to start with a bang and have a great impulse during the first month or two of its career. Certainly, it is an excellent period for dealing with affairs of the army, navy, military engineering, munitions, or with those people or lines of business that deal with heavy muscular or extreme vital energy. It is similarly an excellent period for the building up of a business or interests dealing with iron, steel, cutlery, sharp instruments or things connected with electrical machinery, furnaces and fire.

It is also a fine period in which to deal with enemies, competitors and rivals who have previously been obstacles in your path. But it is a poor time to attempt to master these obstacles or people with arguments or with contracts, papers or agreements. If sheer energy, persistency and long hours of activity and hard work will affect competitors or obstacles in the way, this is the period in which to overcome them in this manner.

It is noteworthy to keep in mind that this is an unfavourable period for men to deal with women and women may keep in mind that it is usually an excellent period for them to appeal to men when seeking favours, preferment or aid in any business or social matter. It is during this period that business strife and many quarrels and arguments occur and these should be avoided because they are not apt to end successfully for any person involved. It is an excellent period for salespersons, lecturers or others who depend upon forceful oratory or fiery argument to convince.

Period No. 4

Period 4 is considerably different from the preceding one inasmuch as in it we have the cosmic forces strongly influencing and strengthening the mental, nervous and psychic side of one's being rather than the physical. It is an excellent period for the writing and mental creation of books, plays, plans, business schemes and other matters requiring a fertile mind, quick thinking, smooth-flowing language and an unusual ability to express the thoughts in the mind. In fact, the mind will seem to be highly charged with new thoughts, new ideas and easily contacted expressions of the Cosmic Mind.

Incidentally it has been noticed that since the mind is very fertile and sensitive during this period, ideas, impulses and urges are apt to flow into the consciousness very rapidly. However, to take advantage of most of these, the person must act upon impulse, quickly grasping the ideas and putting them into practical application before others crowd them out. Therefore, it is a dependable period for acting upon impulses or so-called intuitive hunches. The nature of the person becomes optimistic and because of the mental activity, somewhat nervous and restless, with the imagination being highly charged.

It is a good period in which to deal with literary people, reporters and messengers, to engage stenographers and writers, book-keepers, engravers, artists and people whose work is primarily mental and rapid in expression. Artists are more inspired and more nimble in their work during this time.

A warning must be given here, however. Great deceptions can be practised upon a person during this period. Stories, reports, papers, documents or other written or spoken matters that may come to your attention during this period must be carefully analysed before being accepted. Because it is a period when falsehood is as nimble and eloquently expressed in words or writing as is the truth, deception is not only very easy, but very frequent. Forgeries concerning personal and business papers and counterfeits of important papers or money must be watched at this time. Many of the great losses in life through theft or deception occur during this period, and proper precaution should be taken to prevent these things.

It is a good time for study and for the absorption of special knowledge and for the building up of a quick and nimble mind and tongue. It is not a good time to enter into marriage, to hire people, to return from a long journey or to buy homes, business proposition or lands.

Period No. 5

In Period 5 we enter into what may be called the success period of the year, as far as our personal, private affairs are concerned. During these 52 days, the Cosmic impulses and tendencies are to bring happy fruition and successful termination to the things with which we have been labouring, or the things we have planned or put into action. It is during this time that our personal affairs expand, grow and increase in prosperity. The mind of the person becomes filled with higher ideas of courtesy, religion, science and law and there is a tendency toward good fellowship, sociability, benevolence, honesty and sympathy.

It is an excellent period for dealing with lawyers or judges of the court, government officials, clergymen, physicians, merchants or people of wealth. It is also a good period in which to begin a long journey, contrary to the good period for short journeys which occurs during period 2 of this cycle. It is a very fine period for renewing or starting interests in philosophical works, metaphysical studies, the preparation of sermons or legal briefs, or things requiring very favourable influences to bring to a successful conclusion. For that reason it is a good time in which to collect money that is owing, to buy for the purpose of selling, and to sell, speculate or even to borrow. Any attempts during this period however to deal with tricky affairs that are not legitimate speculations, or to deal with cattle, to buy or sell cattle, to deal with meat products on a large scale or to deal with marine affairs, will prove unsuccessful.

Period No. 6

Here is a period that may be called the holiday of the year. It is a time for pleasure, amusement, relaxation and entertainment. This does not mean however that business will not prosper or that the regular affairs of life should be withheld or modified; for all things that are legitimate and good will continue with almost as much success as during the preceding period. However, it is the time in which to deal specifically with certain affairs of life with more intensity than at other periods.

Now is the time to make long or short visits for relaxation or for the renewing of friendships and it is a fine period for dealing with women, or for women to deal with men in the pleasurable and higher things of life. It is especially fortunate for business matters as dealing with the higher and more pleasant things of life such as with art, music, poetry, painting, sculpturing, personal adornments, perfumes, incense, flowers and so forth. Short journeys will be happy and successful during this time but not long voyages, or in fact any voyages by water.

This period is more fortunate for men seeking preferment, favours or business agreements and co-operation from women, just as the third period of this cycle is more fortunate for women to obtain these things from men. It is a good period also for the consummation of transactions of a speculative nature, or to buy stocks and bonds or to engage employees.

Period No. 7

Period 7 is the critical and disruptive period of life each year. I feel sure that after you have outlined the yearly cycle of your life for each year, if you will then look back over the last 10 or more years of your life and note the things that occurred during the seventh period of each of your years, you will see how true this is. It is a period in which devolution precedes evolution, when a breaking down occurs so that there may be a new building up. It is like the period when the house is torn down, brick by brick and levelled in order to rebuild again.

In one sense it is disruptive and in another, it is the first stage of reconstruction. For that reason, be warned to take advantage of the natural tendencies of this period and at the same time guard against these tendencies so that they may not go too far, or that you do not labour wrongly and run counter to the tendencies instead of co-operating with them. It is the period when most things that have been unsuccessful and are about to end or disrupt, do so.

If a business or any other affair has been going poorly and has shown a tendency to fail and go to pieces, this is the period when such a culmination is most likely to occur. And if this result is not wanted, care must be exercised not to do those things which will help to bring it about. The mind is very apt to become despondent, discouraged or pessimistic during this period and that must be kept in mind; for if this attitude is allowed to affect one's actions in business or in personal affairs, it will help to bring about a disastrous result.

The influences during this period are very subtle and must be carefully analysed and reasoned before being applied. During the fourth period of this cycle, the rapidity with which ideas come to the mind makes it advisable to be quick and even impulsive in accepting and applying the ideas. The very reverse is true in the present period. Impulsiveness here will bring disaster. If matters that are pending or ideas that suggest themselves can be postponed and held over until one is past the coming birthday and then put into the first or second period of this cycle, it will assure greater success.

Period 7 is a good period for dealing with elderly people, judges, referees, or people who must debate and consider carefully and for a long time before rendering their decisions. It is also a good time for business interests dealing with inventions and mechanical things and even for applying for patents or government papers of protection. It is a very good period for dealing in property, mines and minerals and those things that are of the earth and deeply seated in it, or in hidden or out-of-the-way places. For that reason it is a good period to deal with people engaged in lines of business connected with these things, or with grain or fruits of the earth.

Certainly, it is the most unfavourable period in the

whole year for starting anything new, launching a new business, giving a new impulse to something or adding new expenditure in business except for protective purposes. Voyages by sea, long or short, or on land, should be avoided unless their effects are to result in weeks and months in the future when they will fall in another period.

A ND SO WE HAVE the seven periods of cycle two. The influences operating during each of these periods may not begin on the first day of each period, nor end on the last day of each period. In fact, the influences of each period may begin a few days before the period and overlap a few days into the succeeding period. For this reason the precise hour or part of the day in which each period begins is not important.

The only way to be sure that you have the best influences of each period is to avoid the first and last two days of each period in doing anything of a very definite nature pertaining to that period, because at the beginning and end of each of these periods there is a mixed influence of the preceding and succeeding one.

7 Periods of the Business Cycle

With Description of Cycle No. 3

E ARLIER IN THIS book, I stated that everything that has a beginning in the worldly plan of existence starts its career in accordance with a cycle of progression, just as human life begins a cycle at birth. But how long such cycles last or continue to manifest depends upon many things. Just as human life may last for a month, a year, 30 years, or 80 or more years, so a business proposition, an institution or a commercial plan may have a life activity covering a month, a year or many years. However long it may operate or continue to exist, its existence will be in accordance with a cycle of progression that is just as definite as the cycle of progression of human life.

In other words, if several men and women unite today

to organise and incorporate a new business under a new name, to carry on a new line of activity, and the new name of the company and its new plans are adopted and definitely completed today, then this new business would have its birthday today. It would begin its career today and would have a cycle of progression beginning with today, just as though these people had given birth to a human form with a soul.

Each one of our business institutions, business schemes, plans, or forms of activity, has a birthday. In other words, some day in the year constitutes the day on which the business first started, first made its representations to the public or began its material activities.

Most businesses can easily determine what day of the month they began their activities, but the so-called fiscal year should have nothing to do with the determination of the birthday of a business. Many businesses that actually began their careers in June, July or August for example, have made their fiscal year run from September to August, or from January to December. If the beginning of the fiscal year is used as the true birth date of the company, a mistake may be made in working out the periods of each year. It is not absolutely necessary to have the exact date of the starting of the business or proposition, whatever it may be, as long as one can select the day of the beginning approximately. A variation of two or three days will not make much difference.

Now follow a few important points to bear in mind when determining what the true birthday of a business is: The day on which the company received its incorporation charter is not as important as the day on which the company began its business affairs in dealing with the public. The day on which a number of people gathered together and decided to start a business and actually selected the name and officers of the business is a more correct birthday than the day on which the first announcement was made to the public, or the first article was sold. In smaller lines of business, the day on which a store or factory was rented and the work of installing equipment or furnishings was started would be the birthday of the business. The day on which a person gave up his other affairs and began to plan and work out a new proposition would be a more correct birthday than the day on which he actually sold or handled any of the products of his business.

If a business has had a formal opening with a formal announcement of the opening, and a reception of the public, and a definite start of the business in a formal way, then this day would be the birthday of the business. With a business that has changed hands or changed its name, the date on which the firm began to operate with the new name or with the new owners would be the birth date of the present business regardless of how long it had been operating under the older name. So we see that some thought must be given to the determination of what the approximate birthday of a business is.

When we speak of business, we mean not only stores which sell merchandise of any nature at retail but also of factories and manufacturing businesses, brokerage firms, estate agents, professional businesses such as those of physicians, artists, musicians and others in similar lines. A birthday may be the opening of the office of a lawyer or adviser of any kind, or the opening of a mail order or sales proposition, the starting of a canvassing or selling plan, or any scheme or definite operation that has to do with commercial or business activities, wherein either a group of people or only one person is involved.

Having determined the approximate birthday of the business, one should proceed as with the marking of the periods of the cycle of human life. In other words, start with the approximate date of birth and write down on a piece of paper the periods of 52 days each. Let us say that a person or group of persons started the manufacturing of a piece of machinery and that the business was born on the day when the partners gathered and decided to go into business together, depositing their money in a bank and selecting a name for their firm. Let us say that this date was approximately 3rd June. This date each year then would be the anniversary of the birthday of that concern.

Starting therefore with 3rd June, we would count off on the calendar 52 days from 3rd June. This would give us 25th July as the date of the end of the first period and the beginning of the second period. Counting off another 52 days, we would write the end of the second period on the piece of paper and so on until we had written down the dates of the beginning and ending of the seven periods in each yearly cycle of the business.

Now in each of these seven periods, various Cosmic influences, urges, tendencies and impulses would affect the affairs of the business, just as though that business were a human being. Since the business itself depends upon the actions and reactions of human nature on the part of the public and those officers and people directing the business, so we find the business itself reacting to the impulses, urges and tendencies of the complexity of the human natures involved. This therefore enables us to analyse the trend of each business proposition and to discover that it has certain favourable and unfavourable periods during which the best interests of the business may be protected, advanced, modified or conserved.

Let me now present a brief analysis of what each business of any nature whatsoever may expect during the seven periods of its yearly cycle.

Period No. 1

During the first 52 days of the yearly cycle of each business, beginning with its birthday and covering the 52 days following, the business will find greater success in all forms of promotion that solicit or depend for their success upon the goodwill and preferment of the public. It is not as excellent a period for the actual building up of sales and return of money as it is a period for securing approval, favour, recognition and general goodwill.

This would be the period to solicit endorsements or high recognition by eminent people, and concerns that would either result eventually in sales through such people, or in giving widespread publicity and advertising to the concern. It is also an excellent period in which to advertise a business widely, not so much for direct sales as to build up prestige and public recognition.

It is a good period for the sending forth of emissaries, representatives or high members of the firm to meet other eminent people in the business world and therefore secure recognition and high favour. For this reason it is an excellent period to deal with government officials, judges of the court or politicians from whom you desire preferment, special favours or the passage of protective bills or regulations. This makes the period also good for the securing of political influence, political co-operation and recognition. The main concern during this period should be not of money but of name, reputation and prestige.

Period No. 2

During this period, any firm or business of any nature will find that it is a good time to make changes of a temporary nature in regard to important employees, modifications in business practice, temporary locations and for trying out short-term plans and propositions. On the other hand, it is a very unfavourable period during which to make any new agreements, any new plans of a definite nature, or to enter into any contracts or agreements of any kind unless they are reduced to writing and properly sealed and signed so as to give them long-period standing. Verbal agreements and arrangements entered into at this time are apt to be cast aside quickly and changed very rapidly or suddenly and amount to nothing. It is a good period for the building up of business friendships and every business firm would do well to take advantage of this period to contact new and prospective customers in a friendly way, for business friendships of a very helpful nature have generally been built up during this period.

Period No. 3

Here we have a period of construction and great energising power. It is during this period that any business proposition should be pushed to its utmost. Every facility and means of manufacturing, selling, producing, advertising, promoting and extending the business should be adopted and utilised to the utmost during this period. It is also a good period for the arrangement of plans for collections, or to send out collectors or letters intended to collect money. But it is not a good period for attempting to fight any issues in court that have to do with the activities of business enemies, rivals or competition. Other legal matters however, may be pushed at this period and will generally receive more favourable reaction than at any other period, especially if the matter is one that calls for the expenditure of a great deal of energy and of considerable fighting for the protection of certain issues or rights.

On the other hand, every firm and business should watch out for dangerous accidents, disasters and troubles through enemies, fires or sudden explosions of wrath, enmity or hatred during this period. Manufacturing plants and other propositions should be careful of fires or explosions from fires, gases and stored-up energies of any kind during this period. It is during this period also that personal business enemies will attempt to wreck one's business or even to injure the character or life of a person connected with it, if the business has attained any degree of enmity on the part of competitors or others.

It is a very good period for dealing with military matters, the military departments of the government, engineering, munitions, machinery or firms or individuals associated with these.

Period No. 4

This is the period in which any firm or business would do well to enter into its largest campaign of widespread advertising, whether this be nation-wide advertising or the mere solicitation by letter of customers in a limited area. Whatever writing, planning and scheming of promotion that a business firm or individual may want to do in any year of its business, it will be found to be most successful during this period of the annual business cycle of each year. On the other hand, it is also an excellent period for the drawing up of new contracts, new agreements, papers of incorporation, documents, transfers and so forth.

It is an excellent period to deal with journalists, diplomats, arbitrators, or others who can use their mentalities or printed or written words to further the interests of the concern. On the other hand, firms must be careful during this period to watch out for deception by word of mouth or writing, forgeries and tricky agreements or plans cleverly presented and which are apt to have serious reactions in many ways.

Period No. 5

Here is a period of growth and financial success for any concern or business proposition. This is the period in which to seek investment, or to secure credit and extend the time in which payments must be made or negotiations closed. It is one of the best periods in the business year for selling, and the actual distribution of material on a sales basis if immediate results and a quick and fair return of money are desired. It is an excellent period in which to collect bad or old debts and it is an excellent time in which to bring matters to court where the favourable decision desired hangs by a slender thread. For all things being quick and right, this period is favourable to a constructive and just decision.

It is an excellent period also for the promotion of the business into foreign lands or distant places or with large concerns that deal in international matters or have international distribution and sales agreements. It is also an especially good period for business firms to promote their affairs with railway and electricity companies, and with all companies and concerns that deal in things that cater to the pleasures and happiness of the public.

Period No. 6

This is the period in each year when every business should relax its activities if it finds it necessary to relax at all, and should plan its periods for the holidays or absence of any of its important directors or operators. It is also an excellent period for the promotion of certain branches of business such as those dealing with the art world, with music, poetry, sculpturing, artists' materials, women's clothing or articles of adornment, beauty preparations, high grade shoes, hosiery, evening wraps, hats, luxurious cars, oriental rugs, antique furniture, fine books, expensive musical instruments, concerts, operas and other things representing the luxuries, refinements and clean and wholesome pleasures of life. Therefore, it is well to push the sale of things of this nature during this period, or to promote good will or interest among people who are associated with such lines of business.

This is an excellent period for the heads of a concern or the individual owner of any kind of business to make acquaintances with their customers, and to make such intimate contacts with persons as may be helpful to the business or the individuals of the business in the near future. It is also a good period for the collection of money, the buying of stocks and bonds, or the promotion of the finances of the company through investment in conservative stocks of other concerns. Therefore, it would be an excellent period for the bringing about of partnerships, monopolistic corporations and the formation of subsidiary associations and alliances of a similar nature.

Period No. 7

Here we have the reconstruction period for all business propositions and during these last 52 days before the birthday of the concern or business, great care must be taken not to start any new line of activity or to go too heavily into advertising that is intended to build up a new department or a new phase of the business, or to do otherwise than co-operate with the Cosmic tendencies to reconstruct. Since it is the period during which changes of a tearing down nature must be expected, it is a wrong period in which to plan to do reconstruction without the preliminary stage of tearing down. In other words, during this period, no expansion must be expected unless it is associated in some way with a breaking down or tearing down process as a part of the reconstruction.

Since some form of breaking down and change is very apt to take place during these 52 days, every business concern or individual should see that any contemplated changes or tearing down processes that have been in mind are brought to issue during this time and therefore permitted to expend themselves or manifest themselves while such a period is favourable. Certainly, no new alliances, affiliations, partnerships or agreements, contracts or offers of agreement or contract should be made during this period.

It is an excellent time to consult with people in retirement, or who have been in business and have retired, or with judges, referees or advisers of any kind. All acts must be guarded with a conservative attitude, and extreme caution and providence must be manifested in every line of activity. Great diplomacy must be shown in every act, and every business should take advantage of this period to conserve its activities, hold steady to its line of progress and not allow anything of a radical nature in either advertising, selling, buying or planning to occur.

⁓✦⁓

AND SO WE HAVE an outline of the favourable and unfavourable influences, urges and tendencies from the cosmic during the seven periods of the yearly cycle of each business or form of business activity. You may test the occurrences of this outline by going back over your business affairs for several years and noting in what periods of each year you have had trouble with your competitors or with enemies, or in what periods of each year you have had the greatest sales and the most success in promotion, or the most disruptive and tearing down conditions to contend with.

You will soon find, if you review your business activities over a period of 10 or more years, that your business affairs have naturally divided themselves into periods that agree with the outline given above. You will also notice, if you are keenly analytical, that in certain periods of the past when you have attempted to do certain things with your business, your plans have failed or the scheme you had in mind or started did not materialise as you expected. And you will see that it was because you started these things or planned these things in a period that was not favourable.

8

How to use the Periods of the Cycles

IN THE PREVIOUS chapters, two distinct cycles have been outlined. Cycle two, explained in Chapter 6, relates to your own personal existence and explains what tendencies and conditions will be fortunate or unfortunate for you during each of the seven periods that come between your birthdays. Cycle three, presented in Chapter 7, pertains to the career of your business or any venture or proposition that you have created or which has started at some definite time.

If you have your own business or are employed in some business, or venturing into some business, or have some proposition you wish to carry on to success, you will find that you have two cycles to deal with: first the cycle of your own personal life and second, the cycle of the business or proposition in which you are engaged. Each of these two cycles has seven periods to the year and it is not often that the periods of each of these two cycles coincide. If your business or your business proposition was started on your birthday, then its periods each year would run concurrently with the periods of your own personal life. Otherwise, two periods of different conditions will confront you.

For example, let us assume that you were born on 1st June and that the business you are interested in had its beginning around 1st July in the previous year. In trying to find out what you should and should not do in your business and personal affairs during the next 30 or 60 days, you would find if you tabulated the cycle of your business and the cycle of your personal life, that personally you are now in the first period of your yearly cycle, whereas your business would be in the seventh period of its business cycle.

In other words, your personal affairs, tendencies and interests would be affected by the conditions outlined in period one of cycle two, as in Chapter 6 and your business affairs would be influenced by the conditions explained in period seven of cycle three outlined in Chapter 7. In trying to determine therefore what you should do at the present time, you would have to analyse and carefully study the conditions in period seven of cycle three *and* the conditions in period one of cycle two pertaining to your personal life.

Whenever it occurs that the time which you are interested in and about which you are consulting this system, brings your personal life and business life into the same period, then you can easily understand what to do and what not to do. But when the two periods are different and you find opposing influences in each of the periods, you must blend them, analyse them and decide for yourself what to do. It has been found that certain points will be helpful in this regard. If the business you are in is exclusively your own, then you should be guided by the conditions of your personal life cycle as being more important and more dominating than the conditions in your business cycle. But the conditions of the yearly business cycle should always be carefully watched, and the things that are unfavourable therein carefully avoided, regardless of what may be stated in the periods of your personal cycle.

If the business you are in or the business matter in which you are interested is not exclusively your own but is a partnership, a corporation or a combination of the interests of a number of individuals, then you must bear in mind that to make the business succeed optimally, you must follow its individual cycle and periods regardless of your own periods or the periods of other people connected with the business.

There are many times in the affairs of business people when personal desires, personal ambitions, personal success and profits, must be laid aside in order for the business they control to prosper and succeed. In other words, all who have had any real success in business will tell you that very often there have been opportunities, temptations and inclinations in their lives for journeys abroad or long vacations, or other things that would profit them personally, help their health and increase their knowledge and wisdom. Yet, with all of these things coming at opportune times, and with every temptation to yield to them, they have had to pass them by and sacrifice their own personal interests and opportunities solely because business affairs had a different trend and a different set of conditions. On the other hand, it is known that very often when conditions in business are most unfavourable, or seemingly so, there are certain conditions in the personal life of an individual connected with that business that permit him to lay business aside and indulge in his own personal affairs with success and without serious injury to his business interests.

The important point to consider always is whether your individual success, financial progress and best interests in life are so related to your business affairs that both of them will suffer or prosper together; or whether they can be so separated that you individually may prosper while the business may decline and vice versa. Another important matter that must be considered is that in most cases, your personal cycle is of greater importance to you and your connection with the business than the cycle of the business itself. If you are merely an employee in business, then the business cycle with which you are connected is of little importance to you except in so far as you can work with it and help the business by taking advantage of its good periods. On the other hand, if the only business you have is something owned and controlled by you, and is your sole source of income, and you and your family are exclusively dependent upon it, then the business cycle becomes an important matter for your consideration.

If in one period of your personal life cycle conditions indicate that you should exert every effort to build up and create more business, and push your business interests to the utmost, while at the same time the period of the business cycle indicates that you should let your business remain quiet and not push it too strongly, you should use the conditions of your personal cycle to think, plan and create new and better things for your business, but not put them into effect until there is a good period in your business cycle when such things should be done.

Using the system outlined in this book requires a careful mix of the indications given in both the personal and business cycles. It calls for a careful study and analysis of the periods in each of these two cycles, and a proper blending of them until you come to a conclusion as to what you should do and which of the influences and conditions are the most important. Again I would remind you that in the average case, a person's personal cycle is of greater importance than the business cycle, though for corporations or big business concerns where there are a number of men and women owning and directing the business, and where the business is an impersonal one, the business cycle should be given greater consideration than the personal cycle of any person connected with the business.

In all the affairs of the home, of social interests, personal finances, personal plans and progress, the personal cycle is unquestionably the one to be followed above all others.

9 Periods of the Health Cycle

With Description of Cycle No. 4

FOR THOSE WHO want to give special attention to their health during critical periods, or generally throughout the year, this chapter and the one that follows will be of considerable assistance. The health cycle should be mapped out the same way the preceding cycles were by starting with your birthday and dividing each year into seven periods of 52 days each. The conditions concerning health in each of these periods are as follows:

Period No. 1

During this period, the vitality and constitutional health should be at its best, though if it is below normal, it will be more quickly and easily increased and strengthened through normal living and the avoidance of the violation of any natural laws. Plenty of outdoor walking, good air, drinking a lot of water, eating proper foods, and avoiding foods that are overheating, especially the starches and raw or rare meats will yield results. The eyes should be guarded against overuse or use in bright electric lights or sunlight, and if any operation is planned, or system of health building is to be adopted, this is the period in which to start these things.

Period No. 2

This is a period in which many light and temporary physical conditions may affect the body, and passing emotional conditions may affect the mind. In other words, during this period a person may have temporary trouble with the stomach, bowels, blood stream and nerves. These conditions seem to come quickly, last only a few days and pass away just as quickly. None of these considerations however should be neglected, and each should be given immediate attention. However, there is no need for anxiety regarding the continuance of such conditions if immediate attention is given, for all of the influences tend to bring rapid changes in the health and physical condition of the body during these 52 days.

During this period there are apt to be days with headaches, upset stomachs, trouble with the eyes or ears, catarrh, coughs, aches and pains through mild forms of cold, and occasionally with women, aches and pains in the breasts and abdomen. During this period, everyone should try to be cheerful and not permit the mind to dwell upon the temporary conditions that affect the body but simply attend promptly to the checking of any condition that may arise and then cast it out of the mind.

Period No. 3

This is a period when accidents may happen and sudden operations often come into one's life, of both a minor and major nature. Similarly, suffering by fire or injury through sharp instruments, falls or sudden blows, is more likely during this period than any other. People should be careful of their food and not over-eat, and the body should be kept adequately warm for there will be a tendency during this period toward colds, often resulting from overeating or overheating the body.

The blood stream should be kept clean and the bowels active, so that blood conditions will not result in sores, boils, eczema, rash or other more serious conditions of the skin and blood. The blood pressure should also be watched during this period, for there will be a tendency for it to rise, and overwork or strain should be avoided. Any abnormal strain upon any part of the body is apt to precipitate a breaking down during this period.

Period No. 4

In period four, the nervous system of your body will be tried to its utmost and there will be many tendencies toward nervousness expressing itself in the functioning of various organs or in an outer form of restlessness and uneasiness. Too much study, reading, planning or use of the mind and nervous system will surely bring definite reactions during this period. More sleep and more rest are required during this period than in any other part of the year.

Fretfulness and nervousness may also affect digestion and the functioning of the stomach. It may also produce a nervous heart condition that may cause misgivings and inconvenience. People who have been labouring too long or too tediously with mental problems or work requiring mental strain should be forced to relax and rest during this period, or a mental breakdown is inevitable.

Period No. 5

This is another period when the health should be very good, especially if normal living is indulged in and the great outdoors utilised for deep breathing, long walks and good exercise. There will probably be a tendency during this period to overindulge in the things that please the flesh, such as the eating of preferred foods, elaborate meals and banquets, rich concoctions, spicy drinks and so forth, and even overindulgence morally and ethically in many ways. All of this must be avoided during this period in order to prevent serious conditions.

This is a good period in which to recover from fevers, chronic conditions or other abnormal or subnormal conditions of the body that have existed for some time. During this period, mental suggestions, metaphysical principles and right thinking will have more effect upon the body and the health than at any other period.

Period No. 6

This period is another one in which overindulgence should be carefully avoided concerning work, mental strain, eating or any of the pleasures of the flesh. It is a period during which the skin, throat, internal generative system and kidneys may become affected. Therefore, plenty of water should be drunk, the bowels kept open, and rest with outdoor exercise should be indulged in more frequently than mental strain or overwork.

Period No. 7

This is the period during which chronic or lingering conditions are often contracted and which remain a long time and cause considerable trouble in overcoming. Everyone should be especially careful of catching colds or contracting serious fevers during this period by avoiding the places where such things may be contracted. The mind and whole nature is very apt to be despondent and below normal in its ability to ward off and fight an incoming condition. Even the blood stream and immune system will be lowered in their vitality during this period and may therefore be unable to fight even the normal infections or unfavourable influences that generally come in contact with every human being.

However, it is also not a good time for taking medicine, having an operation performed or for starting any new or drastic method of improving the health unless in an emergency, or it is to be continued over a long period so that its real effect will come into the next period of 52 days, which will be period one of the next cycle. The eyes, the ears and in fact any one of the five senses may become affected during this period, and care should be taken that colds or other conditions do not linger or continue without expert attention. It is one of the most serious periods of the whole year for each person with regard to diseases and chronic conditions.

10   *Cycles of Disease and Sex*

A S STATED PREVIOUSLY, the laws and principles set forth in this book have nothing to do with the art and practice of astrology. Whether or not one believes that the planets have any effect upon life is immaterial in consideration and application of the system set forth in these chapters.

The influence of the moon upon plant and animal life has been in considerable dispute and I believe most of us have read books arguing for and against such a claim. However, many observations indicate that by noting the lunar cycles and the rhythm of the periods of the moon, we cannot help coming to the conclusion that there is at least some influence measured by the periods of the moon which does affect animal and plant life.

We are certainly able to notice a rhythmic periodicity in connection with diseases, fevers and some normal functioning of the human body related to the psychic side of our beings, and which are coincident with the rhythmic periods of the moon. Whether this relationship is merely incidental and of no importance, or whether it establishes and proves a great universal law, I will leave for you to determine. I must call attention however to the fact that the psychic and emotional sides of our being are closely related to the origin, development, continuation and final ending of all diseases, abnormal mental and psychological conditions, and other so-called involuntary activities of the human body.

I probably need not call your attention to the interesting observation that has always puzzled psychologists, psychiatrists and others, namely that those who are suffering from a temporary or prolonged abnormal mental condition seem to have periods of stress, quiet action and reaction, in keeping with the periods of the lunar cycle. The ancients noticed this so long ago that the term "lunatic" was brought into use under the belief that the moon (luna) was responsible for the abnormal mental states of human beings. Many of the more subtle and vital activities of the inner or secret organs of the human body are unquestionably associated with the psychic nature of the human being and are also associated in some way with the moon.

So true is the association of the lunar rhythm with the

manifestations of many of the psychic and more subtle effects and conditions of the human body that the periods of these conditions are measured by the moon periods of approximately 28 days each.

While all this is generally admitted by most people and by medical researchers, and is undoubtedly seriously considered by true students of nature, the relation of such a rhythm to the phases of the moon is not generally known. Scientific discoveries have confirmed many of the principles that have been known to Rosicrucians for centuries and are still used by them in many ways.

As a planet, the moon has a very definite cycle of phases, the cycle covering a period of approximately 28 days and known as a lunar month or lunar cycle. Because this cycle is divided into phases and these phases are further divisible, I will divide the lunar cycle into discreet rhythmic units. Half the moon's cycle is approximately 14 days. Half of this (i.e. ¼ of the cycle) is about 7 days. Half of this is about 3½ days, or 84 hours.

The full lunar cycle, consisting of one complete revolution from perigee to apogee and back again to perigee, is the lunar month. This complete cycle is often referred to as the *long cycle* of the moon, while a *short cycle* would be the ordinary tide cycle corresponding to the upper and lower transits of the moon. This short cycle is on average 12 hours. So we have two moon cycles to refer to: the short one of 12 hours, known as the moon's tide cycle, and the long one of approximately 28 days. We are of course dealing with averages here because of slight variations in time.

Because there are long and short *cycles*, we will have long and short *units* of these cycles. Not as an arbitrary matter but because of fundamental laws that you will recognise, we will call the 3½ days arrived at above the unit of the long cycle, or a *long unit*. Taking the short cycle of 12 hours and dividing it by 4, we can define 3 hours as a *short unit*. A long unit of 3½ days equals seven short cycles, or 7 x 12 hours, giving 84 hours.

The two units arrived at above, one of 3 hours and one of 3½ days, manifest themselves in the rhythmic actions of the mind and body like waves or undulations of a rhythmic nature. Here is where we make important discoveries and can

Typhoid Fever	7 - 21 days	2 - 6 long units
Varicella	14 days	4 long units
Smallpox	7 - 14 days	2 - 4 long units
Scarlet Fever	3½ days	1 long units
Measles	10½ days	3 long units
Whooping Cough	10½ days	3 long units
Dengue	3½ days	1 long units
Diptheria	3½ - 10½ days	1 - 3 long units

augment the findings of science through our other knowledge of certain laws of nature.

In the case of diseases, we find some very interesting and helpful facts by analysing average cases and using the averages of units of the moon's cycle. These averages betray the effect of anabolic and catabolic lunar phases or units of the cycle as shown in the incubation periods of the following diseases.

In all acute fever cases of any name or nature, the rhythmic period of these units is very pronounced and definite. Regular changes occur every seven days (as has been noted for years) or in other words, after every two long units (one positive and one negative, as we shall see). The longer the disease continues, the more definite are the changes every seven days and even the single unit, 3½ days, is well marked and important.

These units of rhythm also manifest in the process of germination and gestation of life, and can even have the effect of determining sex. The average time in hatching eggs of many species is 3½ days or one long unit. In many insects, it is 1½ weeks or 3 long units. The hen lays eggs for 3 weeks (6 long units) and sits on them after this for an equal period of time.

In human beings and many other forms of life, each sex possesses an equal number of chromosomes but the gender chromosomes (XX) are alike in the female and unlike in the male. The female egg contains 22 autosomes plus 1 X chromosome. The sperm are of two kinds: half of them carry 22 autosomes plus 1 X chromosome; the other half carries 22 autosomes plus 1 Y chromosome. The Y chromosomes are diminutive. When two X chromosomes come together at fertilisation, the offspring is a girl. When X and Y chromosomes come together, the offspring is a boy. The difference is in potentiality or polarity.

Returning again to the short cycle of 12 hours, called the moon's tide cycle, we find that the action of the tides gives us the key to the potentials. The 6 hours of time preceding the maximum point of high tide are strengthening and the 6 hours immediately following the hour of high tide are weakening in their effect on the psychological and psychic or emotional processes of life. The 3 hours immediately before high tide are positive hours or constitute a *positive short unit* (or wave) of the rhythmic cycle. The 3 hours immediately after high tide are negative and constitute a *negative short unit*.

Each positive unit is preceded by a negative unit and followed by a negative unit. Hence every 12 hours constitutes a tide cycle, with two positive and two negative pairs of units. In each 24 hour day, there are therefore four such positive and negative pairs of units. But to determine when a pair is negative or positive we must take the hour of high tide as the starting point, taking the hour of high tide as it is known for

Chart C

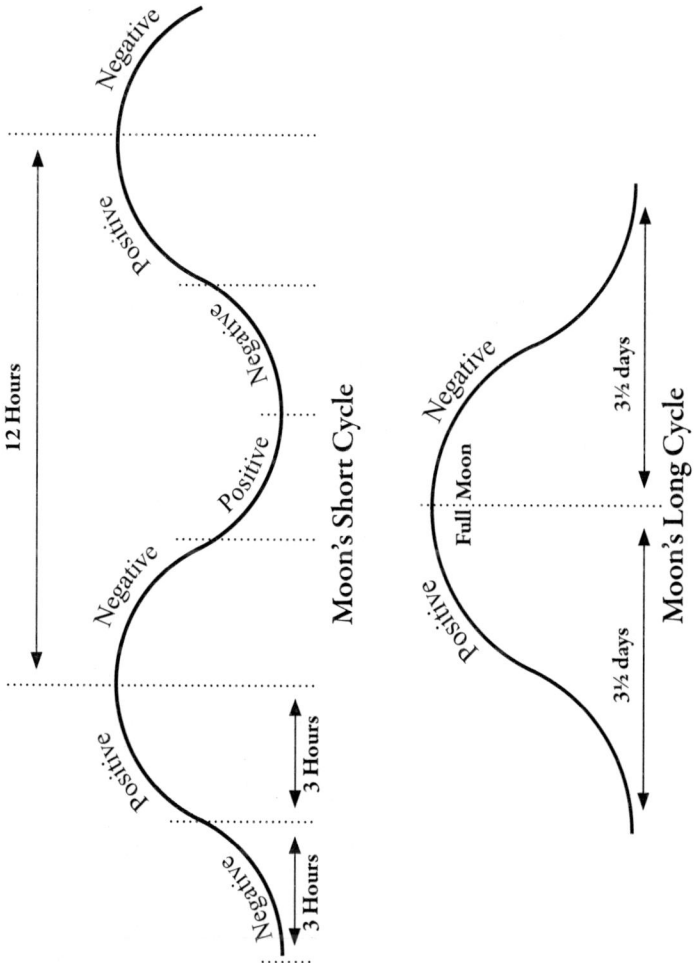

Moon's Short Cycle

12 Hours

Negative

Positive

Negative

Positive

Negative

3 Hours

Positive

3 Hours

Negative

Moon's Long Cycle

Negative

Full Moon

Positive

3½ days

3½ days

each locality on the face of the earth, regardless of whether the locality is near a body of water or not.

Taking the long cycle or lunar month cycle of an average of 28 days, we have the long unit of 3½ days. There are eight of these long units in each long cycle (8 x 3½ = 28 days). We find that the first of these units immediately preceding the hour of full moon is a positive long unit and the unit following the full moon is a negative unit. Hence we have 3½ days before full moon as positive in nature and 3½ days immediately following full moon as negative in nature. There are four such positive and four such negative units of 3½ days in each lunar cycle of 28 days.

It is easy to see that in addition to the cycles explained in previous chapters, we are living under the influences of a very systematic though strange series of alternating psychic units of positive and negative rhythmic waves, some 3 hours long and others 3½ days long. Therefore, while one of the long positive units of 3½ days is in effect, there will be 28 short units of 3 hours each, alternately negative and positive in effect also. A positive short unit in effect during a positive long unit will give a very positive effect. A negative short unit in effect during a positive long unit will give a neutral condition. A negative short unit in effect during a negative long unit will give a decidedly negative condition.

The long units of 3½ days have their greatest influence on the purely psychic functioning of the organs or psychic processes during illness or abnormal conditions of the body. The short units have their greatest effect on the mental, nervous and biological functioning and processes of the body in either health or disease.

It is for this reason that the long periods have an important effect on such illnesses as already mentioned and many others, while in conditions such as fertilisation, fecundation, contagion and similar processes, the shorter units have a greater effect. A purely positive unit or period of time produces a strong, life-giving, masculine condition, while a purely negative unit or period produces a weaker, feminine condition. The one is active, the other restful. The neutral period, as mentioned above, produces a passive condition.

We find the short units exerting their influence very strongly in the conditions relating to childbirth. Here the nervous system, the sympathetic processes and the organic functioning, are very sensitive to the influences we have been describing.

During the negative long unit of time, especially the first three hours after high tide, the body is at rest and contractions are weaker and less helpful during labour. The positive long unit, especially the first three hours immediately preceding high tide, produces an active condition as far as contractions and other conditions are concerned, and the patient needs less wilful effort and is less likely to need external or artificial assistance from a doctor. If the birth does not occur during the first two units (six hours) preceding high tide, it will not occur without forced and painful conditions during the next three hours (the first unit after high tide) or without unnecessary suffering and weakness during the next three hours (the second unit after high tide). The patient should be permitted to rest during the negative units and become active and helpful only during the first unit before high tide.

Note that the labour contractions are rhythmic and become stronger during the positive units of time and passive or weaker during the negative units. By taking advantage of such influences on the rhythm, the patient retains much strength, the use of drugs is minimised and artificial assistance is entirely avoided. Of 100 tests made by this method, 98 confirmed each principle involved and the other two were affected by other causes and conditions of abnormality.

In thinking, planning, talking or doing any mental or functional act requiring strength of the nervous system, impressiveness or personal magnetism and good vitality, take advantage of the positive units of time. In the treatment of disease, administer all help possible during the long positive units and the short positive units but permit the patient to rest during the negative periods. If a crisis is due during a long negative period, keep the patient as quiet as possible until a positive unit is at hand, especially a long one. Then, if the patient has not succumbed, the positive unit will assist in passing over it successfully.

To properly determine the units of time, you should secure from an authentic source the daily or weekly schedule of tides for the city or locality where you live. Similarly, locate a moon table such as is published in most almanacs, giving the revolutions or phases and cycles of the moon for each month.

IMPORTANT

ALL THAT HAS been learned or revealed by experiment regarding the moon's cycles is contained in the previous pages of this chapter. Neither the author nor the publishers can attempt to give to individual readers any information regarding the moon's periods and influence upon tides for various localities, nor the moon's probable cycle of influence in connection with various diseases and illnesses.

Whatever indefiniteness or incompleteness there may be regarding the moon and its influence in such matters is a problem awaiting further study and investigation at the hands of the new scientific age. Let us hope that the rising generation, becoming free of the bias and prejudices of the past, will undertake this great work.

11 The Daily Cycles of Significant Hours

HERE IS ANOTHER important cycle that will probably be used by the readers of this book more frequently than the other cycles because of its timeliness and the ease with which it may be consulted concerning many occurrences of the day.

I know of thousands of business men and women who have used this cycle in an abbreviated form as a guide to their affairs, and who consult it during the day in connection with every important matter that comes upon the horizon of their business or personal affairs. We have tested this cycle in thousands of ways and all who were fortunate enough to know of it report that it is one of the most dependable guides ever used by them.

This cycle divides the 24 hours of the day into seven equal periods of approximately 3 hours, 25 minutes and 43 seconds. The daily cycle begins at midnight, ends at midnight, and noon of each day is the centre of the cycle. The first period of the cycle is from midnight to 03:25; the second cycle ends at 06:51; the third cycle ends at 10:17; the fourth cycle ends at 13:42; the fifth cycle ends at 17:08; the sixth cycle ends at 20:34 and the last cycle ends at midnight.

As stated in previous pages, the use of the periods of the various cycles must always allow for variations of a few minutes, hours or days at the beginning of each cycle. In using cycles two and three, a variation of a day, or at least of a few hours, must be allowed at the beginning and ending of each of the periods. The full effect of the conditions pertaining to each period of any of these cycles does not become manifest until the period is fairly well established.

In the case of the present cycle, no matter where you live, you should allow five to ten minutes at the beginning and ending of each period for the conditions to become established. Therefore, although the cycle ends at 03:25 in the morning and the second begins at that moment, it is safer to consider that the first period ends at 03:20 and the second period begins at 03:30. This leaves a neutral period of five to ten minutes at the end and beginning of each period, when the full effect of the condition allotted to either period may not be manifest.

The value of the daily cycles becomes apparent the minute one attempts to use the system. Testing it for a few weeks will give better warrant for its use than any argument I may present in these pages. Those who feel reluctant to guide their lives and daily affairs by any mechanical or strange system like this need not feel that there are any superstitions connected with it. A superstition ceases to be a superstition as soon as the principle behind it becomes manifest and the operation of the principle proves the existence of a fundamental law.

While some may argue that the use of such systems as these is the result of faith or belief in them, the fact remains that such faith and belief are natural results from the discovery that the law is workable and works even in the lives of those who know nothing of this law. As I said above, it hardly behoves me to spend time arguing the benefits to be derived from this system, for it takes only a few weeks of test and trial to demonstrate the law that is in operation behind it.

Before attempting to use the daily cycle, the following chapter dealing with the complete instructions for its use must be carefully read. Once these instructions are understood, it will be a simple matter to refer to the periods of the daily cycle any hour of the day and be guided by the information given. It may be somewhat new in the lives of many people, but if stockbrokers and those in the business of stocks and bonds and the fluctuations of stock markets find it profitable to consult a system like this, and if the heads of big corporations find it helpful to consult this system in their daily affairs, certainly every business man and woman will find it pleasant, interesting and profitable to consult the clock and periods in this book, just as the captain of a ship consults his maps and various guides each hour of the day and night.

12

How to use the Daily Cycle of Seven Periods

A S STATED IN the previous chapter, this cycle divides the 24 hours of each day into seven periods. Each period is approximately 3 hours and 25 minutes long. The periods begin at midnight and end at midnight.

Please note however that the periods of each day are not identical in significance. For instance, the first period on Sunday is quite different in significance from the first period on Monday. And the fifth or sixth period on a Tuesday is quite different from the fifth or sixth period on a Wednesday, or any other day of the week. All the periods of Wednesday for instance are the same for *every* Wednesday but they will not apply on the other days of the week. The same thing may be said of any other day of the week.

The charts given in this chapter make this very plain and easy to understand. The illustration given here of a 24 hour clock, shows the day divided into A.M. and P.M., with the seven periods of the 24 hours marked on the dial of the clock (Chart D). Note that midnight is at the top of the dial and noon is at the bottom and the hours on the left side of the dial are P.M., while the hours on the right side are A.M. This clock enables you to see at a glance the hours in each of the seven periods, from midnight to midnight.

We are going to name these seven periods by the letters A, B, C, D, E, F and G, just like the notes on a piano, or any other musical instrument. No doubt you know that the letters of the musical scale run from A to G and begin with A again. The seven periods of the 24 hours of the day run in the same manner.

In using this daily cycle for any day of the week, look at Chart E, "Periods for each day of the week" and note what periods for the day you are to consult. Then turn to the list of daily periods and read the description that fits. For example, suppose it is Monday and you want to know the best things to do and what things you should avoid doing during the early business hours. By turning to Chart E you will see that 08:00 on Monday morning is in the third period of Monday. Therefore, it is in Monday's "E" period, while midday on the same day is in Monday's "F" period. By turning then to Chapter 13 and reading the description of these daily periods, we turn to the period for "E" and note what conditions are propitious at that time and what conditions or

Chart D

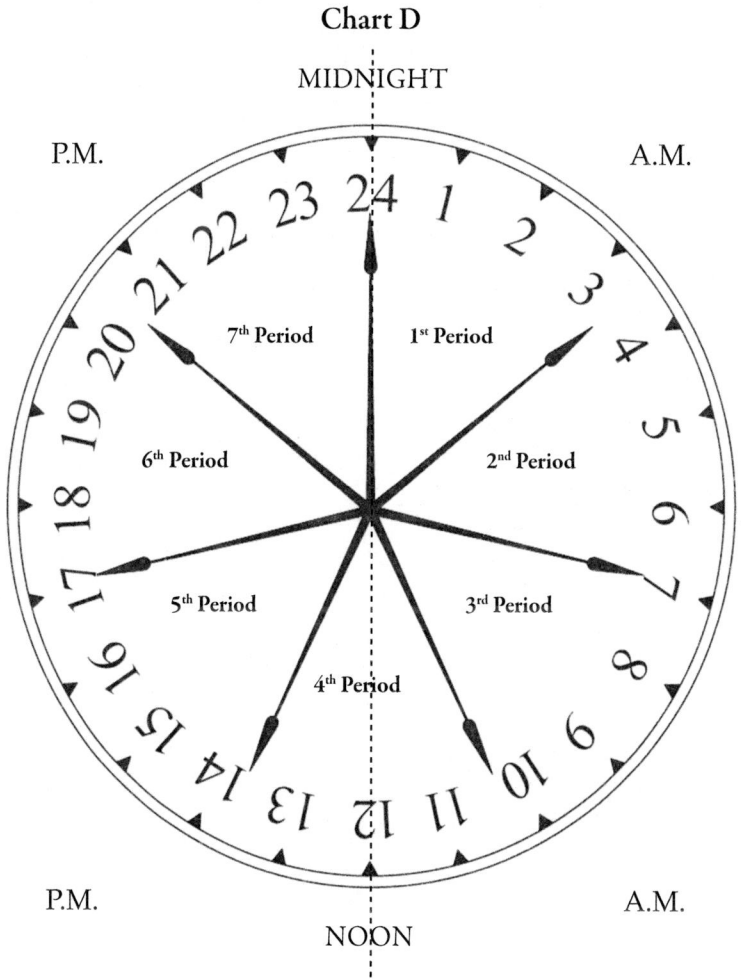

MIDNIGHT

P.M.   A.M.

7th Period   1st Period

6th Period   2nd Period

5th Period   3rd Period

4th Period

P.M.   A.M.

NOON

Chart E
Periods For Each Day of The Week

Time Period	Sun	Mon	Tue	Wed	Thu	Fri	Sat
No. 1 Midnight to 03:25	G	C	F	B	E	A	D
No. 2 03:25 to 06:51	A	D	G	C	F	B	E
No. 3 06:51 to 10:17	B	E	A	D	G	C	F
No. 4 10:17 to 13:42	C	F	B	E	A	D	G
No. 5 13:42 to 17:08	D	G	C	F	B	E	A
No. 6 17:08 to 20:34	E	A	D	G	C	F	B
No.7 20:34 to Midnight	F	B	E	A	D	G	C

tendencies should be avoided. We may do the same thing for the "F" period of Monday.

Let us take another example. You may be planning to visit someone on a Monday evening around 20:00 to discuss business matters. By turning to Chart E, you will see that 20:00 on Monday evening is in the sixth period of the day and that it is Monday's "A" period. By referring to the description of the "A" period, you will notice that it is an excellent time in which to ask favours and to solicit aid and help from prominent people of high position and so forth. But you will also notice that this sixth period of the day ends at approximately 20:34 and unless you can present your proposition and get action on it before then, your discussion of it will run into the seventh period and that period is the "B" period of Monday.

This is good for visiting and social affairs and pleasantries, but not so good for the business purposes you have in mind; therefore, your business proposition may be postponed or set-aside until some other day. This warns you to try seeing your important friends earlier in the evening but not before 17:30, for that would be too early for the sixth period to have become fully established.

Note that although 17:30 to 20:30 is in the "A" period for Monday, it is in the "D" period for Tuesday and in the "G" period for Wednesday. If you wanted to find another suitable "A" period during which you might bring your business solicitation before some important person or group of people, you would have to wait until the third period of Tuesday morning, roughly between 07:00 and 10:15, or the "A" period of Wednesday, which would be roughly between 20:40 and midnight.

As another illustration, let us assume that you are anxious to find the proper period or periods of the week in which to collect or invest some money, or you wish to start a new move or plan or proposition which you hope will be a financial success. By reading the descriptions of the day periods, you will discover that the "F" period of the daily cycle is a good one in which to do the things you are planning to do in connection with financial matters. Now, by consulting Chart E you will note that there are seven "F" periods in the week.

The first one is during the seventh period of Sunday from 20:34 to midnight; the next one is during the fourth period of Monday, from 10:17 to 13:42; the next is in the first period of Tuesday morning, midnight to 03:25; the next is in the fifth period of Wednesday, from 13:42 to 17:08; the next is the second period of Thursday, from 03:25 to 06:51; the next is during the sixth period of Friday, from 17:08 to 20:34; and the last is during the third period of Saturday, from 06:51 to 10:17.

In choosing the best of the seven "F" periods, or any other of the lettered periods of the week, two points should be kept in mind. First, those that are late at night or very early in the morning must be eliminated because of the impossibility of using these midnight hours for general purposes. Second, one should be guided by the best periods for the particular thing to be accomplished, bearing in mind that several of these lettered periods may serve the purpose, rather than only one. In the illustration just given of the "F" periods, we find there are seven periods that you can use for your financial purposes and of these seven, the best ones to use would be the "F" period of Monday, which is during the mid-morning business hours, or the "F" period of Wednesday, which is early afternoon, or the "F" period of Friday, which is roughly between 17:10 and 20:30.

The next important way in which to use these daily periods is as follows: Suppose someone comes to you with a business proposition, a plan, a request, a demand, or a suggestion of some kind and you find yourself becoming interested in what is proposed or required. Before taking any action on the matter, you should immediately turn to the description of these daily periods and to the table to see what period of the day you are in, and note whether it is a propitious time for the matter in hand.

Suppose the person who has come to you has a contract, agreement, lease or some paper to sign. Glowing terms and promises are being expressed to you and you have been swayed by oratory, fine words and fine arguments. But when you turn to the charts in these pages, you find that the matter has come before you on a Monday morning, at 09:30. This is the "E" period of Monday and is generally not a good period for signing papers, contracts or agreements and not a good period in which to place any faith in the spoken promises and glittering word pictures of anyone. In this way you will be warned not to enter into the matter but to dismiss it.

Even if you attempt to hold the matter off until the next period, which is an "F" period and therefore fortunate for financial matters and for contracts and papers, you will not help matters, since the matter actually had its birth and its start in your interests during the "E" period. By your voluntary postponement of it you will not help yourself, for that would be establishing an artificial condition. If, on the other hand, the person who proposed these things to you had come to you during the "F" period instead of the "E" period, you could have felt that it was safer and more dependable.

Let us also suppose that this person had presented these matters to you on Friday at 11:30. By reference to the description of the lettered periods of the day, you would find that this "D" period of Friday at 11:30 is not a good time for the making of agreements, contracts or investments that are to last for any length of time or have any degree of permanency to them. Therefore, you would refuse to enter into the proposition and would dismiss it.

Bear in mind that once a matter is dismissed by you

because it has come to you in a period that indicates that it is not safe or good, it should never be taken up again at any other period. To attempt to do so would be to frustrate the principles of this system and set them aside entirely. If a proposition comes to you at a period that indicates that it is not a good thing for you to enter into, its merits will not be changed by having it come up again during another period. One cannot imagine a mining proposition that is thoroughly unsound or a speculative business proposition that has no foundation to it, being radically changed and made safe and sound overnight by delaying the presentation of the proposition a few hours. The significance lies in the period in which it comes to you *for the first time*. A proposition may be perfectly safe for others to invest in or to consider or co-operate with, but for you it is not safe, good, propitious or fortunate and this is signified by the time in which it first comes to your attention.

Therefore, you will be justified in setting it aside permanently, even though others who hear of it at a more propitious time may find it good for them and go into it. If you are to get any benefit out of this system at all, it must be remembered that the system in each application is representing you and your best interests and not necessarily the rest of humanity.

A person may come to your home or office with some proposition at 10:00 in the morning and because of the hour and the period, you find it advisable to reject it as being unfavourable or unfortunate. The canvasser however, may walk to another street and present the same proposition to one of your neighbours. During the time of his walk, the third period of the day has ended and the fourth period has begun, and so the canvasser approaches your neighbour in an entirely different period than the one in which he approached you. The fourth period may be a propitious or fortunate time for the proposition he submits. Therefore, your neighbour would be warranted in accepting it, whereas you rejected it.

This does not show a weakness or an inconsistency in the system. We all know that there are propositions that are fortunate, helpful and worthy of consideration on the part of some people, while the same things are unfortunate and inadvisable for others. One person can invest money in a certain proposition and make money out of it, while others who invest in it realise later that it was not a fortunate thing for them. This system, therefore, is consistent with the varied conditions that surround each individual and helps to explain why there are such inequalities and unequal opportunities and advantages for human beings.

By carefully studying and analysing the matters set forth in Chapter 13, describing the lettered periods of the day, you will become familiar with those things which should be undertaken, planned or started, and those things which should be avoided or dismissed during the different periods. Therefore, you should watch the hours of each day in your office, business or home affairs and act accordingly.

One interesting point should be emphasised here. It appears from a long test of this system by people who have kept accurate records of the results, that the more urgent the proposition which a person is considering, and the more vital it is to his personal or business affairs, the more important it is to him to consider the period and act accordingly. In other words, the more trivial affairs of social and business life, or the mere routine matters of daily business and social affairs may be carried on safely without consulting this system. But to the same degree that any matter is of vital moment and calls for careful judgement, careful analysis and considerable thought, an intense consideration should be given to the system and the period of the day. Surely in any matter that is of utmost importance, where the decision or choice will bring lasting and serious results for either good or bad, it is far better to consult this system and be guided by it than to depend upon hasty judgement, the toss of a coin, or the acceptance of an urge that may be a temptation or an external suggestion from some other mind.

As stated in an earlier chapter of this book, urges, inspirations, temptations and impulses to do things or to hesitate in doing things come to us from the cosmic and from the minds of people around us, and very often there are two impulses, two urges, two arguments or two tendencies and we must choose between them and accept one or the other. Here is where you can exert your privilege as a free agent though you must ever abide by the result of your decision. It is far better therefore to place your dependence in a system like this than to depend exclusively on your objective analytical ability, or on any rational system of thought or analysis.

This system has been tried and tested and proved to be in accordance with a set of higher laws that most people neither understand nor are interested in. But its simplicity, wide range of adaptability and power to give confidence, warrants its uses. Give it a chance, for you can make of it a real silent partner in all your affairs.

13 *Description of the Daily Periods*

THE SEVEN DAILY periods have their qualities in much the same way that the annual periods do. What follows now is a brief description of the qualities of each one.

"A" Period

Many things may be done during this period of the day, with the hope of fortunate realisation and Cosmic co-operation. For instance, one may concentrate or meditate upon any plan for the purpose of evolving its details. You may ask favours from people in high positions, especially when such favours relate to a promotion in position, in political power, or in social position. You may ask for stays in legal proceedings, the loan of funds, the endorsement or recommendation of a proposition, or a much needed introduction to a certain important person.

This is a propitious time for dealing with public officials or people of high rank. It is also ideal for the signing of wills, deeds or transfers, the writing of important letters that seek favours, promotions or recommendations, or which carry to the mind of another person a high regard of one's self, one's business, or any plan one is proposing. It is a good time in which to talk to bankers or financiers for the purpose of building up personal credit or the credit of a business, the making of a public appearance or address for the purpose of bringing esteem and honour to yourself or your business, or for building up your reputation or the reputation of your affairs.

It is not a good period in which to deal with criminals or evil matters, even as a lawyer or adviser. It is a time filled with energy that must be controlled. It is also a period filled with fiery impulses that must be governed, just as all words and acts must be cautiously controlled. It is not a good period to start a new business, a new plan or a new proposition of any kind. It is not good for the buying of livestock, and neither is it good for the signing of contracts or agreements.

It is not a good period in which to start short journeys of a few days' duration, nor is it a good period in which to deal with marital affairs or to marry or to go courting. It is a bad period in which to borrow money, to move into a new location for either home or business, or to start the erection of a new building of any kind. And it is not a good time in which to make the first financial investment in a new business. It is not fortunate for buying real estate or even for selling or renting it. Nor is it a good period for surgical operations.

"B" Period

This period is fortunate for the following things: Matters dealing with art, music, the beautifying of the home or person, or with matters pertaining to purely material and sensual affairs. It is an excellent period for starting any new undertaking; for the enjoyment of art, music and drama; for the buying of livestock; for the collection of accounts; or for dealing with the public in connection with public administration, public affairs and public utilities, or soliciting business from the public. It is also good for the hiring of agents, collectors, travelling representatives, salespersons and employees for important positions in the business or home.

New acquaintances made during this period are generally dependable and worthy of friendship and trust if they come into your life purely in a social way. It is a good period to start short journeys lasting only a few days, but certainly less than a month. It is a good time for marriage and courting, for lending or borrowing money; for putting into material form any new plans for business or pleasure; for indulging in recreation and social affairs; or for holding any social function. It is a good period for seeking social or business favours and is also good for speculating, for games of chance and for investments of a speculative nature. Finally, it is a good period for dealing with women in either business or social matters.

It is not a period of great ambition, and while quite changeable, it is easily adapted to many conditions. It is a fruitful period inasmuch as most things started or culminated during this period will be more prolific than one may anticipate. It also brings its impulses of an intellectual and social nature, which must be guarded against. It is not a good time for hiring people for menial positions and is not a good time for starting long journeys, especially those by train, water or air that take one far from home.

"C" Period

This period is especially fortunate for dealing with the fine arts, or the intellectual things of life, especially education, scientific research, publishing, printing, instructing in schools, colleges, universities and in the promotion of campaigns involving an educational element. It is a good time for study, memory work and absorption of special knowledge, analytical examination of documents, books, papers and propositions, or to deal with legal arguments in court requiring the use of the intellect and logic. It is an especially good period for mental activity of any kind, including writing, thinking, speaking and self-examination. It is also a good period to indulge in drama, music and art.

The buying of livestock or dealing in cattle or the livestock market, is fortunate during this period. It is a good time for the making of contracts providing they are not for long periods but of short duration. It is also good for the collection of accounts, the making of new, dependable acquaintances and the hiring of business employees and servants of all kinds. It is a good time to start short journeys, to do literary and newspaper work, prepare advertising, start new advertising campaigns, or to send out literature to the public pertaining to business or social affairs.

It is a good time for the taking of medicine or any system of therapeutics that is to benefit the physical body. Although it is a favourable time to lend money, it is questionable whether it is a good period in which to borrow. It is a good time in which to erect new buildings or to plan new undertakings, and students of the occult, the philosophical and metaphysical will find that this is an excellent period for study and objective realisation of great truths.

It is a good period in which to take a chance with undertakings that are tricky or questionable from a financial point of view, though only for one who has the means to do this without bringing financial embarrassment should the result not be all that is expected. It is a good period in which to have a few minutes of recreation or social intercourse and for signing important papers of all kinds, and it is similarly the best period for travelling salespersons to call upon the most difficult of prospective customers. It is also a good time for writing important letters.

This period is not so good for dealing with enemies or bringing them to court, or attempting to adjust matters with them, for there will be endless discussions and arguments without any beneficial results. It is quite a changeable period in many ways, giving great mental activity but not enough prudence and caution, and no dependence should therefore be placed on one's usual cautiousness. It is not good for marriage and it is a questionable period to deal with lawyers concerning any problem, to deal with inventions and mechanical problems, to seek promotion in business or to ask for the favour or recognition of public officials or prominent people. It is not a good time to buy property and it is questionable whether it is a good time to sell property. It is a doubtful period for seeking favours or for spiritual development or concentration and is an unfortunate period for dealing with surgeons or having a surgical operation of any kind.

It should be remembered that during this period one encounters an increased nimbleness of mind and tongue. Any person presenting a proposition or plan to you is apt to exaggerate or mislead through biased statements or evidence. Forgers, blackmailers, liars and people who are deceitful, are apt to appear during this period. Therefore, guard yourself accordingly.

"D" Period

Here we have a period that is especially fortunate for all general material affairs of business, dealings with the public in any general capacity, educational work of any kind, planting or farming operations, the making of new acquaintances and the hiring of employees.

It is also a good period in which to start short or long journeys by water, and for writing, supervising or dealing with literary or newspaper work. It is a good period for marriage or for courting, for all marine affairs, for the taking of medicine or any system of therapeutic assistance for the body or mind, for metaphysical study and analysis, or for dealing with shipping and transportation interests or the actual shipping of goods to places out of the city in which you live. It is also good for dealing with surgeons or for surgical operations, and it is one of the good periods for salespersons, travelling agents and others to solicit and sell and especially for dealing with women. It is a period in which the ambitions may be highly aroused, and while these ambitions may be very impulsive, they will generally prove fruitful.

It is not a good period for commencing any new undertaking, the buying of livestock, the making of contracts, or the signing of legal papers of any kind, or to start litigation or court actions. It is not a good period in which to borrow or attempt to borrow money, nor sign any papers or notes pertaining to money matters, nor speculate, nor take part in games of chance of any kind. It is also a bad period for writing letters, pleas or requests of any kind asking for important favours or aids in connection with business, personal or social life.

"E" Period

This period is particularly good for aggressive pursuits, or those activities that require deep thought followed by a long campaign or a long period of steady action, and it is good to begin these things during this period. It is an excellent time to have one's affairs come before judges, referees, magistrates, police authorities, senators, governors, mayors or the presidents of large corporations, or those who have within their power the privilege to decide or render decisions in any matters of dispute. It is a good period for bringing permanency to anything started or finished during it and gives great persistency and endurance to all activities.

It is also good for literary or newspaper work or for advertising or sales promotion by mail using letters or brief printed communications. It is also good for starting any legal action in court, or for the submission of briefs or arguments and for all inventions or mechanical problems or matters dealing with them; also for matters pertaining to metallurgy or affairs with metal workers. It is a good time to move into a new house or to buy and sell real estate or to move into or transfer real estate. It is an excellent period for starting or indulging in scientific pursuits and for spiritual meditation.

This period however, is also unfortunate for certain things, and these are quite definite; and it should be noted that the unfortunate things will prove to be very unfortunate indeed. They are: The making of contracts or agreements of any kind other than the purchase of homes; attempting to collect money, the planting of seeds or starting of farm operations; making new acquaintances for the first time; the hiring of agents, salesmen or collectors of any class or for any position; or for starting long journeys.

The period is also very unfortunate for journeys by water, or for marriage; or for the taking of medicine or any method of mental or physical cure; for borrowing or lending money; erecting new buildings; dealing with public officials or prominent people from whom you seek personal favours or special recognition; starting any risky business; indulging in recreational or social affairs; speculating in business or in the stock market; for surgical operations; or for writing letters of an important nature.

"F" Period

This is one of the most fortunate periods in each day. It might be called the lucky period, just as the preceding one is generally considered the unlucky period. During this "F" period of each day, conditions are ideal for the starting of any new undertaking, the buying or marketing of livestock, either in speculation or for actual business purposes, for making contracts or signing contracts, agreements and all papers of specific stipulation, for collecting accounts or raising money for educational work and educational interests, for making new acquaintances, or starting long journeys, either for business or pleasure.

It is also a good period for short journeys by water and other means, for literary and newspaper work, for dealing with lawyers, for the submission of briefs or papers to court, or the actual starting of court proceedings. It is also good for marriage or courting, for borrowing money, erecting new buildings, working out the plans of new undertakings and holding directors' meetings for the discussion of business conditions or new ventures, for seeking promotion in business or the building up of trade and credit reputes, dealing with public officials or with the public in all affairs, or with prominent people.

It is a good time for the buying or selling of real estate, for all social affairs and recreations, for seeking favours, especially for women who are seeking favours from men in either business or social matters, and for signing papers dealing with important matters of any nature. It is a good period for all forms of speculation, and for the writing of important letters.

A few things should be noticed concerning this period

however. It brings a great deal of energy to the body and mind and tempts one to overdraw in many ways; and yet with all the impulsiveness of this period, it is generally fruitful and therefore fortunate. In business affairs, it is a more favourable period for men than for women, whilst in social affairs it is more favourable for women than men.

It is a period of positiveness and yet with a natural tendency toward caution and prudence. It generally gives and begets the spirit and love of justice, and the period makes for permanency. It is not a good time for hiring people for any menial position, nor is it good for marine affairs.

"G" Period

This period is especially good for mastering those affairs that require considerable energy and aggressiveness, endurance and persistency. It is an excellent period for dealing with matters requiring the expenditure of more physical than mental energy, things that require real labour and muscle. Therefore, all material and sensual affairs will be fortunate during this period, as well as the collecting of money, the hiring of travelling salespersons, agents or collectors, or the soliciting on their part.

It is fortunate for marital affairs, marine affairs, the working out of mechanical problems, inventions or building plans, or matters dealing with metal and metal workers. It is also good for scientific pursuits and for women who are seeking favours from men in social or business affairs.

It is not a good period for any beneficent matters, or matters dealing with the receipt of gifts or favours, or public humanitarian activities. Nor is this period fraught with much prudence and caution. It is an unfortunate period for the buying of livestock, or speculating with them, or for dealing with enemies, or for starting long journeys, or for legal actions, or dealings with lawyers or matters in court.

Naturally it would be a bad period for marriage or for courting and seeking favours generally. It is very questionable whether it is a good period for surgical operations or for men dealing with women. This is the period in which accidents are apt to occur. Therefore, one should be careful about being in any place of hazard or being near firearms, fire, explosions or other things that would affect the physical body. In illness, fevers are apt to be high during this time and the body is naturally warmer during this period than at any other.

14 *The Soul Cycle*

I N PRECEDING CHAPTERS we have spoken of the existence of cosmic vibrations and emanations throughout the universe and the effects that these have upon the personal affairs of human beings through the tendencies, urges, inspirations and conditions they create or stimulate in our daily lives. It should be apparent to anyone who analyses the principles involved that these cosmic vibrations and rhythms would have some effect upon the soul-personality and character of each human being.

As stated before, the ideas contained in this book and the various systems presented have no relationship with the postulations and principles of astrology. But if the soul entering each human body at birth is an essential part of the cosmic energy or cosmic vitality, and if this energy or vitality reaches the earth's surface in rhythmic pulsations of energy, then a person born during any specific rhythmic period of the year should have tendencies different from those possessed by a person born during a different rhythmic period. I will not explain how and why this is so, but present instead the *effects* of such rhythmic pulsations upon the soul and character of classes of individuals and allow your own observations to establish the existence of this law. Those who wish to devote their time and study to a deep investigation of the principles involved will find in the work much knowledge and happiness.

Passing over the laws or principles therefore, we come to the observed facts and note that the solar year of 365¼ days may be divided into seven distinct periods constituting the *soul cycle*.

In the northern hemisphere, the solar year begins on or about 22nd March, when we have that distinct astro-phenomenon known as the spring equinox, signifying in all countries of the northern hemisphere, as in ancient times, the birth of a new year. The establishment of 1st January as the beginning of a new year is a purely arbitrary thing and has no foundation in natural law. The solar year is a fraction more than 365 days in length but for all practical purposes we may take the year as being 365 days. If divided into seven equal periods, we find that once again we have a periodicity of 52 days and a few hours. We may ignore the fraction of a day in each period and make each period an even 52 days.

Therefore, we begin the soul cycle on 22nd March and divide it into periods of 52 days each as follows: From 22nd March to 12th May; 13th May to 3rd July; 4th July to 24th August; 25th August to 15th October; 16th October to 6th December; 7th December to 27th January; 28th January to 21st March. Each of these periods has a dual polarity and we find that the first half of each period produces a slightly different effect from the last half. Therefore, we have seven periods, each having two natures and producing a total of 14 distinct natures or combinations of conditions.

Now everyone who is born takes the first breath of life and breathes into his or her system the cosmic energy that starts up the soul consciousness of the being, in attunement with the cosmic vibrations and rhythm existing at that time. According to ancient observations which have been verified through centuries of careful examination and scrutiny, each person continues vibrating in attunement with the rhythm established at the moment of birth. Each person becomes an affinity of the rhythmic conditions existing at the time of birth and therefore, is continuously more sensitive, receptive and responsive to the effects of that rhythm than to any other. It is as though various notes on a perfectly tuned musical instrument were being played at different hours of the day, and a person who was born just as the note "A" was being played would for life be responsive to and affected by the sound of "A" or the vibrations of the note "A" to a greater degree than to any of the other notes played in the entire octave.

In fact as individuals, we are more attuned to certain musical notes or chords than others, and that is why some pieces of music, which have our natural note more dominantly expressed than other notes, affect us strongly. Every created material thing has its musical note, whether it be a glass pitcher or goblet, a chair, a mechanical device or a copper pot. The note with which it is attuned is its natural note and there are therefore certain harmonics of this note that have effects upon it also to a lesser extent and in a different manner. If a harmonic of the true natural note of a glass vessel can be properly played upon a violin string for instance, it may either cause the glass vessel to shatter to pieces, or it may have some other effect upon it according to which harmonic of the natural note is played. All of this however, deals with principles other than those covered here.

In outlining the system of the soul cycle, we observe that the seven periods with two polarities to each of them, give us 14 combinations of notes or rhythmic pulsations which produce certain definite characteristics, tendencies and elements in the personality or soul consciousness of each individual. It is my purpose to outline each of the 14 periods, so that the reader may have a true character analysis of the inner nature or soul-personality of every person he or she contacts.

Before beginning to outline this system with the various descriptions, I must call your attention to the following important points. It must be kept in mind that the cosmic effect upon the soul consciousness of each person does not always manifest itself in the outer, objective nature of an individual. The inner personality of people we meet may be very different from the outer individuality or character. In many cases only intimate, friendly relationships over a long period of time will reveal to us the true inner nature of a person whom we thought we had understood very thoroughly.

The outer, objective mind and character of a man or woman may clothe them with certain tendencies, habits, expressions and mannerisms which they may have assumed or acquired, or even put on for various reasons and which may not be truly consistent with the inner self. The various systems of character reading, such as palmistry, physiognomy, phrenology, handwriting analysis and so forth may be a fair index to the characteristics of the outer self, with occasional points relating to the inner self. Yet all those systems fail to give us a true picture of the inherent, deep-seated, soul personality.

Very often, we find through character analysis of the outer self that people whom we meet are in different occupations, professions, avocations or social positions than we expected to find them, or anticipated. We then discover that the system we had used for such character reading was only an index to the changing, objective outer self, and because this outer self is vacillating and has the power and privilege to assume and affect temporary conditions, mannerisms, choices of professions and occupations, we can place no dependability upon the system we have used. Whenever we use this system however, which gives us an index of the inner nature of any person, we find upon close questioning and intimate association with that person, that regardless of the person's outer life and characteristics, inwardly, privately and in seclusion, the person lives true to his or her inner index and cosmic soul nature.

Furthermore, it avails us very little to become thoroughly acquainted with the outer character and nature of any individual. As far as any benefit being derived from knowledge of the outer nature of a person is concerned, it is just as safe and serves as good a purpose to take people as we find them outwardly and casually. Very few people are capable of concealing their true outward natures. An acquaintance with anyone for 24 hours, which would include casual conversation with her and an observation of her activities in business or home life, will tell us as much about her outer habits and outer characteristics as any involved system that has ever been devised. Knowing the general outer objective, material traits, habits and characteristics of a person does not in any considerable way give us an advantage, benefit or protection. A person who is a thief outwardly and in all of his habits, cannot conceal that from the careful observer. It is the person who is inwardly a thief, a cheat and a deceiver, while outwardly posing as honest, dependable and reliable, that must be guarded against, and against whom we must be protected and warned.

In all social and business relations, the real value of character analysis or intimate acquaintance with personality, must relate to the true self within and not to the fictitious, temporary, vacillating, inconsequential outer self. If we would know whether it is safe to trust another person with our secrets, our money, our confidence, our association, then we must know the real nature and personality within, regardless of the artificial or temporary characteristics of the outer self. If one would know whom to select for a partner in business or marriage, whom to select as a friend or companion, or to perform an important errand or commission, or to fill an important position or place of authority, one must judge by the true inner nature and not by the temporary nature of the outer self.

If one would know one's friends better and understand their moods with the resulting fancies, foibles and tendencies, one must know each person's real self and disregard the outer self. If parents want to understand their children and help them to develop along the lines that originated as natural cosmic tendencies, and which will keep them in attunement with the cosmic personalities born within them, resulting in greater happiness and success in life, the parents should have an intimate understanding of the inner natures of their children. In so doing, they should disregard the passing characteristics that impinge themselves upon children as a result of casual association, imitation of another's habits and similar external influences of a temporary nature.

And above all else, if you wish to know your real self and learn why there seems to be a constant conflict between the changing desires and wishes of your outer self, and the natural tendencies that urge from within, and thereby make the best of your life in all affairs and in every situation, you should know with what tendencies, abilities, characteristics and strong points of personality you were born, and thereby become acquainted with your inner self.

The following index to soul character and personality will do all these things in a different manner than any system of character reading has ever done before. However, just because the indications and index of characteristics given pertain to the inner self, be warned against what may seem to you to be contradictions or inconsistencies.

You may be tempted to use your own life as the first example with which to test this system. You may select your birthday from the table of periods published and discover in what period and what polarity of the period of the solar year you were born. Then, turning to the descriptive index for that period, you may read that you have characteristics, tendencies, faculties and abilities that seem different from those you thought you had. As you can't match what you think you know about yourself with what this book says you should know, you may be inclined to dismiss this system as either incomplete or unreliable. But many who have profitably used this system for years already, would say to you: *"Are you really in a position to know what your real, inner characteristics are?"*

No doubt your response would be to say that you have often thought about yourself, noticed your natural habits, and carefully analysed your inner hopes and desires and should therefore be in a better position than any other person to know your inner tendencies. Remember however, that until you have thoroughly analysed yourself over a period of many years, and have carefully tabulated, without bias, prejudice or personal interest, the strong and weak points of your character, you cannot be a proper judge of the real nature that was born into you at the time of your birth.

You will find that you will do better in testing the system to read the inner characteristics and nature of someone with whom you have been acquainted over a long period and with a few of whose inner, personal traits you have become acquainted. If you are able to judge the other person without a personal interest and without personal bias or prejudice, you will be able to discern that person's subtle and minute traits of inner character better than you are able to judge your own.

The real value of this index is that it enables the honest investigator of his own inner self, or of the inner selves of his children and friends, to help strengthen the inherited birthrights that are good and overcome those that are unfortunate or undesirable. In other words, this index should become a guide to character building and the moulding of a more ideal and perfect personality.

Accepting that each one of us is born with certain tendencies, natural abilities and special faculties, it is certain that the best of these, or those that are good and useful, will become a greater asset to us if developed than any abilities or capabilities we may arbitrarily assume to be ours, and artificially create in our own lives.

Let us say for example that a certain woman's inner nature is revealed in the index as being that of a natural healer or physician and that she has certain cosmic tendencies and abilities for healing which, although part of her inner nature, remain dormant, awaiting development, application and usefulness. Let us also assume that not knowing of this natural tendency of her inner nature, she arbitrarily selected as her profession that of architecture, because of acquaintances she had in that profession and because of another inner, natural tendency toward art and drawing.

To become a proficient architect, she has to create and build up a faculty or ability that was not naturally born in her, and this effort requires years of study, along with years of patient practise. Even so, she cannot attain in her profession of architecture that success, prosperity and renown that would have come to her if she had become a physician.

She would find that to become a proficient physician she would have had to do less studying, less concentration upon the development of her abilities, and less striving after the success she sought. As an architect, she might attain a reputation as a careful, conscientious and mechanically exact worker. As a physician however, she would have attained a reputation for being an inspired, natural, prolific and wonderful healer. There would be that difference between her work as a physician and her work as an architect that is noticeable in the work of the great masters in art, music and the sciences, which comes from inner inspiration and so-called fortunate inheritance.

Another person may have an inner, natural ability for writing and for the beautiful expression of thoughts in impressive language. Not conscious of this natural tendency, he may become a painter or musician by arbitrary choice, or because within him there was also the cosmic urge to express himself in the finer arts. To become a proficient musician or painter may require many years of study and practice, accompanied by years of privation, bringing fame and fortune to his name only after he had passed away.

As a writer however, he would have found his pen and mind becoming more facile and prolific in expression, with less study and less practice than art required. And he would have found success early in his life and would have lived to enjoy the fruits of his divine inheritance. As a writer, he would have been recognised as an inspired thinker, though as an artist or musician he would have been classified as mediocre, or perhaps simply as a successful one who had battled against the odds of life to attain recognition.

In other words, the faculties and tendencies that are our divine inheritance through cosmic direction at the time of our birth, are the things that we may easily develop and apply in our lives to attain success, happiness and prosperity, and at the same time contribute to the needs of humanity and the benefits of civilisation.

It would therefore appear that each of us is born to fulfil certain niches in life and to carry on definite missions in connection with certain lines of work and labour in our earthly lives. We hear so often of the born musician, the born artist, the born business person, the born creator and thinker, and others who seem to have come into this life with certain abilities well established and well developed. Such people are those who have learned or discovered in some way their true inheritance and natural birthright. They have been permitted to develop along these inherited lines and to become successful in expressing them for the benefit of others.

A musician may be born in a family of carpenters and a great architect may be born in a family of farmers who have never had even a primitive realisation of architectural design. A great musician may be born in a family of people who have never heard good music, and had no opportunity of judging between good music and that which is otherwise. Nothing can explain this great diversity of natural tendencies, except the cosmic law of divine inheritance. That in some cases a carpenter may have a son who becomes even more successful than himself in that trade, or an artist or musician may have a son or daughter who follows successfully in the same line, in no way warrants the belief that physical inheritance alone determines the natural tendencies and attributes we find in all human beings.

In the following chapters therefore, a complete system is offered to you whereby you can analyse and study the inner, natural, inherited tendencies, abilities and traits of character of any man, woman or child. Again, a note of warning must be sounded concerning the differences in the stages of evolution to be found in human beings.

It has been proven that there is no such thing as racial supremacy. Those of any race, given equal opportunity and advantage, will display in one or more generations intelligence equal to any other. This has been shown in the case of individuals whose parents and grandparents lived under the most primitive conditions. When the offspring were reared in a higher civilisation and given an advanced education, they attained success in intellectual capacities.

Remarkable accomplishments however on the part of what were once erroneously called inferior cultures, when given the opportunity to develop their natural tendencies, plainly indicate that neither race, religion or colour have any bearing upon the blessings that each human being may receive from the cosmic. And this should make all of us more tolerant and sympathetic in our thoughts of those in other lands and among other cultures, who may not have the advantages we have, but are nevertheless equal with us as children of God and recipients of the cosmic benedictions.

15 *How to Determine the Periods of the Soul Cycle*

I N THE FOLLOWING pages, you will find an outline of the seven periods of the soul cycle for the solar year. Every person's birthday comes within one of these seven periods, each of which is further divided into two polarities, an A and a B polarity.

The first period of the soul cycle is from 22nd March to 12th May which is divided into two polarities. The A polarity is from 22nd March to 17th April and the B polarity is from 17th April to 12th May. A person born on 20th April would be in the B polarity of the first period of the soul cycle. A person born on 3rd December would be in the B polarity of the fifth period of the soul cycle. A person born on 21st March would be in the B polarity of the seventh soul cycle.

Those who are born at midnight on the division of any period will have to be judged by a combination of the indications given for both periods. For example, a man who was born at midnight on 15th October would have his birthday on the precise division between the fourth and fifth periods of the cycle. Therefore, to judge his inner character, a blending of the B polarity of the fourth cycle and the A polarity of the fifth cycle would have to be taken into consideration. All seven periods end at midnight and begin at midnight on the days indicated and the same is true of the A and B polarities. A person born at midnight on 8th June would be in the second period of the cycle, though in reading the description of the character and personality, a blending of both the A and B polarities of the second period would have to be taken into consideration.

The hour of birth has nothing to do with this system, except as it pertains to the midnight hour as stated above. The place of birth has nothing to do with the system either. The year of birth is of no importance, for the periods in the cycle are the same year after year. It is better not to attempt to analyse the characteristics or personality of a person when the precise birth date is not known, unless of course, it is known to be within two or three days of the centre of one of the polarities of the periods, when a variation of a few days will not make much difference.

Perhaps you will accept one other little word of advice. Those who are using this system may from time to time copy from

Chart F
Periods and Polarities of The Soul Cycle

PERIOD No 1:	**22 March**	**to 12 May**	
Polarity A	22 Mar	to 17 Apr	
Polarity B	17 Apr	to 12 May	
PERIOD No 2:	**13 May**	**to 8 June**	
Polarity A	13 May	to 8 Jun	
Polarity B	8 Jun	to 3 Jul	
PERIOD No 3:	**4 July**	**to 24 August**	
Polarity A	4 Jul	to 31 Jul	
Polarity B	31 Jul	to 24 Aug	
PERIOD No 4:	**25 August**	**to 15 October**	
Polarity A	25 Aug	to 20 Sep	
Polarity B	20 Sep	to 15 Oct	
PERIOD No 5:	**16 October**	**to 6 December**	
Polarity A	16 Oct	to 11 Nov	
Polarity B	11 Nov	to 15 Oct	
PERIOD No 6:	**7 December**	**to 27 January**	
Polarity A	7 Dec	to 1 Jan	
Polarity B	1 Jan	to 27 Jan	
PERIOD No 7:	**28 January**	**to 21 March**	
Polarity A	28 Jan	to 23 Feb	
Polarity B	23 Feb	to 21 Mar	

this book a description for some person and give it to them as a helpful guide. When doing so, it is best not to call the written description a *life reading* or a *horoscope*, or any similar term that may be misleading, but call it instead a *Soul Reading from the Cycles of Life.*

This will distinguish these descriptions from astrological readings with which they have no connection, and with which they should not be related even in the mind of a person who is not familiar with any of these systems. It is my wish to keep the systems in this book clearly distinguished from all others, as they have been in my own personal use for so many years. You will generally find that your friends and acquaintances will appreciate the knowledge that the description you give them is from a different system and resulting from a unique method that is free from any superstitious beliefs or undesirable principles.

16 *Description of the Periods of the Soul Cycle*

Period No. 1
22nd March to 12th May

THOSE BORN between 22nd March and 12th May of any year inherit from the cosmic a very lofty nature, with a deep seated desire to achieve a high place in the esteem of the public and in the hearts of their closest acquaintances. They carry over from their previous incarnations the lessons and tribulations that have taught them the necessity of looking above and beyond the commonplace things of life and holding a vision of the highest ideals as their goals. They also carry into this life recollections of the experience of having achieved a notable place or position in life in some foreign land, and having tasted of a full cup with many of the luxurious and beautiful things of earthly existence.

Therefore, in this incarnation, no matter in what station socially or financially they may be, there is always the inner urge to try to live a noble life, or at least one that will be above the commonplace, and that will bring them the respect and perhaps the adoration of the multitude. There is not just a desire for wealth or the material luxuries of life, although there is a taste for these things slightly beyond the average. But the great desire, the great longing that actuates these people in their subjective thinking and planning is the attainment of public renown and public approval.

For this reason, these people reluctantly deal with sordid things and constantly struggle against things that are mean, lowly or objectionable to good taste and high ethical standards. This means that if they started this incarnation or the lessons of this life in a lowly social or financial position, there will be a continual restlessness and dissatisfaction that urges them onward and upward. They always sense the nobility of their last life. They are generally trustworthy, for they have learned in the past that deceit, falsity, underhandedness and unethical practices hold them back in the progress they wish to make. Their words are generally their bonds and their aspirations are not dreamy or mystical, but practical, and adhere to a straight line of progress.

There is of course the natural tendency carried over from the past to want to rule and dominate, and therefore to be the heads or leaders of any plan, organisation or group of interests with which they are connected. In such capacities they will succeed because of their other inherent qualities. They are generally careful in the selection of their words and the use of language in writing, and have commanding personalities when allowed to develop properly, as well as well-developed dramatic faculties. Such people are usually affable among their peers, with perhaps a slight tendency to be impatient with those who do not aspire to rise, or who may be classed in their subconscious minds as the lowly serfs of a past kingdom.

These people can always be reached and appealed to through suggestions of sumptuousness and magnificence and whatever may be honourable. They will succeed best in business matters where they are managers, directors, controllers or overseers, mayors, governors or any high governmental officer, or holders of important positions in the courts of law. In more humble positions, they will succeed as sheriffs, magistrates of small courts, or executive positions of a similar nature.

They have an excellent preparation and faculty for the study of law and in an artistic manner, they are fond of metals and working in metals, not as jewellers but as designers and creators of beautiful and magnificent things of metal. As second choice, they would succeed as designers and creators of magnificent buildings or arrangers of beautiful homes, or the creators of beautiful costumes and articles of adornment.

The physical weakness they have inherited in this life are affections of the heart and brain, perhaps through mental overwork and tendencies toward weakness of the eyes and toward fevers. They will find joy and recollection of familiar things from the past by travelling in countries covering ancient Chaldea and Phoenicia, as well as Italy, Sicily, Switzerland and Scotland.

Polarity A
22nd March to 17th April

Those born in the first half of this period, from 22nd March to 17th April, will be more active in fighting their way to the top of the ladder of their ambitions than those in the B polarity. They will use all their vital energy and power, and every physical means to achieve leadership and dominating positions, and will be like warriors in mastering and controlling any situation or line of work with which they are connected. Their constitutions will be fiery and strong and their personal magnetism well developed, with excellent speaking voices and commanding writing styles.

Polarity B
17th April to 12th May

Those born in the last half of this period, from 17th April to

12th May, will have greater tendencies to seek the goals of their ambitions in the fine arts or in the more refined and delicate places of life. They will be more genteel than those in the A polarity if given the opportunity to develop their inherent tendencies, and will be more subtle, more smiling and quieter in their achievements of success than those in the A polarity. Nevertheless, there is the same determination, with an additional characteristic that some may call bullheadedness. These people will often be associated with art, drama and music, either as hobbies or as professions if they have the opportunities to allow their natural tendencies to guide them.

Period No. 2
13th May to 3rd July

Persons born in this period come into this life carrying from the cosmic and from their previous incarnations, memories of many peculiar experiences, tendencies and characteristics that make strange combinations. In the first place, they bring into this life from the past a deep-seated desire to travel and move about, for they have been successful and happy in this in a previous life. The continuation in this life in any one place or in any one line of thought, or in any one hobby for a long time spells monotony to these people. And however they may try outwardly to associate themselves permanently with some place or set of conditions, the inner restlessness causes them to feel uncomfortable and to seek a change. In one of their incarnations they have been not only experienced in journeying but in exploring, investigating and in trying to taste all phases of life.

What they associate themselves with is generally of a more delicate, refined and temperamental nature. They have inherent desires to be well mannered, thereby expressing tender natures, and the wish to be well received and well considered. There is a cosmic desire to search for novelties and the passing pleasures of human life that are wholesome and yet filled with joy and happiness. But there is another equally strong desire, carried over from an old incarnation by each of these people, to occasionally delve into the sciences and the more practical things of life, and these two desires constitute the strange complex that occasionally manifests itself in their lives.

They are practical, saving, conservative in many ways and yet always of the present hour. They have a tendency to let the future take care of itself because of their faith in the just reward that will come. They prefer to live free of the cares of life, seeking peace and quiet whenever they are troubled. They are not easily led into quarrels, arguments or disagreements and love to spend time in meditation. In many affairs, there is a tendency to be fickle, or so it would appear at least from the outside, whereas in truth it is only another form of the expression of the desire for change and for new experiences.

They are honest, careful, ethically precise in many ways,

and clean and wholesome in character, but are apt to be misjudged because of their changeable natures. But these people must guard against being led into the company of those who seek only the pleasures of the flesh, for once they are started on a downward path, they become heavy drinkers and are beggarly, careless and given to disregard the niceties of life.

In the trades and professions, they succeed well as travelling representatives, or people connected with business affairs that require changes of location and contact, with many branches and fluctuating interests. There are inherent faculties and abilities that will make them excellent secretaries, designers, artists, salespersons, actors or actresses, concert entertainers, newspaper reporters, or servants in fine homes. A peculiar tendency on the part of these people is that of marrying people who will bestow titles upon them or will bring changes of position into their lives. Very often the women marry men who look upon them and treat them as queens or as countesses and pay continued adoration to them, whereas the men often marry women who are well-to-do and who look upon their husbands as kings in the homes.

The inherited physical weaknesses give a tendency toward troubles with the bladder and toward rheumatic diseases, colds and coughs. Often these colds will manifest through a disturbance in the stomach or in the feet or eyes. These people find joy and interest in travelling through such countries as Flanders,

Norway, Denmark, Holland and Belgium, where they will contact sights and conditions familiar to them from the past.

Polarity A
13th May to 8th June

Those born between 13th May and 8th June, have quick intellects and are apt to enter into businesses that permit them to use their minds and fingers rather than all of the muscles of their bodies. In other words, quick minds, quick tongues and quick hands will serve them unusually well, and they are apt to be employed in two occupations or have two hobbies and interests at the same time and to give the impression to others that they are almost dual in their manner of living and expressing themselves.

They should do everything in their power to develop the intellectual and mental side of their lives, because of their inherited mental faculties. People in this polarity will make themselves known by their intellectual pursuits and will be credited with excellent education and training, even if they have not actually had them in any school or university.

Polarity B
8th June to 3rd July

Those born between 8th June and 3rd July are generally outstanding characters in the intellectual world, for they continually associate themselves with those interests or industries that deal with education, the fine arts or the law. Their intellectual capabilities are more reserved and must be discovered, and they usually manifest in excellent memories, fine appreciation of language, intuitive senses that enable them to foresee and prophesise or perhaps sense oncoming conditions before anyone else may think of them. They are somewhat more stable in their physical changes of location, although the love of travel and of change of residence causes them to move occasionally. However, they will vacillate more in their intellectual pursuits and in their reading and studying than in their physical environment. They are able to serve as secretaries or associates in business to a greater degree than those in any other period or polarity.

Period No. 3
4th July to 24th August

Those born between 4th July and 24th August of any year carry from the past into this life the experiences of great struggles and achievement through determination and self-mastership. In other words, we have in this period those who are already potentially self-masters and masters of fate. They have a strong constitution, a fiery, impetuous nature and the will-power and ability to accomplish against great odds, if there is sufficient motive and some encouragement.

In addition to this inner nature which is a part of their

soul consciousness, their birth during this period have given them from the cosmic other related faculties and abilities which will enable them to be bold, confident, invincible characters in the achievement of any great purpose. These people will challenge any obstacles that may arise in their lives, even though outwardly they may not realise that they have been stirred to action or aroused to a fighting spirit by obstacles that others may have looked upon as insurmountable or perhaps insignificant according to their natures. In other words, this is the type of person who can be encouraged and led into action, when presented with an obstacle, as being one that others have failed to overcome. Naturally, these people are lovers of contest and seekers of honours in contests, not merely for aggrandisement but because of the mastership it will establish.

They are apt at times to be boastful of their abilities and this demonstrates a weakness that must be overcome. They never hesitate to risk life or limb or their best interests to achieve anything that they believe was destined for them to master, whether in association with their own personal interests or not. Naturally, if carefully placed and properly trained, these people become great leaders in movements or employment calling for the use of strong will-power, strong hands and strong principles. If allowed to have their own choice in professions, they will invariably succeed as captains or officers in the military, or as leaders of great movements calling for strong, masterful leadership.

In positions that are more conservative, they will succeed as surgeons or chemists, or even as carpenters and contractors. They bring over from their past an inherited inclination and liking for the making of small things of an intricate and mechanical nature and they are therefore often inventive and successful in such lines as watch-making, electrical design or the making of small mechanical devices of a very important nature.

Their physical weaknesses may manifest in the tendency toward diseases of the blood, carbuncles, ringworm, eczema, sores of the skin, yellow jaundice and similar conditions. There is also a tendency toward trouble from gallstones or burning fevers and they should be very careful with their diet for they are apt to eat highly seasoned foods and too much meat. We will find them attracted to and interested in such places as Lombardy, Batavia, Northern France and Paris, for there they will recall conditions that seem familiar.

Polarity A
4th July to 31st July

Those born between 4th July and 31st July are apt to be adventuresome and to travel a great deal, seeking adventure and doing things that call for the risking of life and limb. They are therefore natural explorers and investigators. If unable to travel considerably, they will explore even in their own immediate country and be known by their restless desires to delve into the mystery of conditions that baffle the conservative nature of a person who is not so ready to risk his life.

These people make good leaders of armies, or leaders of naval forces and they are often associated with political or reform movements for they love conquest and can carry an issue to victory. They often lead double lives in many ways, for they will have many interests and two outstanding occupations or methods of applying the faculties of their natures.

Polarity B
31st July to 24th August

Those born between 31st July and 24th August generally succeed in achieving the attainment of some position that places them at the head of some great organisation, as in some high political office equivalent to that of a governor, mayor, judge or president. They are naturally royal in their instincts and habits and love pomp and ceremony, limelight, adoration and approval of the public. They live their lives in keeping with these desires and therefore carefully guard their weaknesses and those habits which might jeopardise the high positions to which they aspire; for they learned this lesson in a previous life

In any occupation, whether on the stage, in literary work, in business or in social affairs, those in this polarity are leaders or outstanding characters, and mediocre positions in life will not satisfy them. Children born in this polarity should be given every form of education and training that will enable them to hold high positions with efficiency and with honour to themselves and their parents.

Period No. 4
25th August to 15th October

People born in this period carry into this life, from a previous incarnation, the attainment of high personal powers, positions of leadership that have to do with education, the fine arts and especially the development of civilisation and the best interests of the public. Together with these characteristics, such people have received from the cosmic the additional benefits of wonderful faculties for study and the attainment of knowledge and the ability to express themselves in words or writing together with very fine memories, the ability to reason logically and to live a life of aestheticism if the opportunity is afforded.

These people are hard to become acquainted with objectively, for their intellectual abilities and knowledge enable them to clothe themselves with the colours of their environment and to meet people on their own level. We may find them in the most humble positions of life, seemingly occupied with pursuits and affairs of a lowly type and yet, through acquaintance, we discover that they are truly prepared and trained for higher and better positions than those in which we find them. On the other hand, we may find them in the highest positions of the literary world, or at the head of educational institutions where they give more thought to the advancement of humanity than to their own advancement.

The cosmic rhythm has created in them a natural desire for learning and research, and they are very fond of mysteries, whether in fiction or in actuality. These people also have the tendency to appreciate the power of words and the finer points of law and scientific knowledge. There is a tendency toward searching into the occult and into the secret and arcane wisdom of all ages, as well as into philosophy and religion, though in the latter sense, the tendency is toward non-sectarianism and the building up of universal brotherhood and love.

They are very capable in trade or business, and make excellent merchants because of their ability to read human nature and to understand the desires and wishes of others. For that reason they make good salespersons, good instructors of sales forces, or writers and editors of advertising and sales literature. Their ability to reason logically and to express their ideas with logical arguments make them qualified for many positions where this natural ability can be used. Their abilities often lead them into politics where they succeed well, but not to the same extent that they would in some truly humanitarian profession.

They have also often acquired considerable advancement

in metaphysical and occult illumination in a previous incarnation, and very often they were formerly adepts in one of the arcane mystery schools such as the Rosicrucian Order. There is something about their soul-personality development and spiritual attainment that makes them truly great masters inwardly, and they are restless and unhappy until they contact in this incarnation that place or point in their soul progress where they left off in the last incarnation.

These people should be guided to the Rosicrucian work or some similar course of study and development at an early age, for that will be the beginning of another phase of rapid progress and development for them. Honour, temperance and mystical idealism, accompanied by an unusually wonderful imagination, are the keynotes of their real inner characters. We find them often occupied in the present incarnation as literary workers, mathematicians, secretaries, writers, sculptors, poets, orators, school teachers, college professors, bankers, clergymen or ambassadors.

The physical weaknesses which are subtle physical tendencies of their natures, generally express themselves in dizziness or brain fatigue, accompanied sometimes by a slight degree of stammering or imperfection of enunciation, due to the attempt at rapid expression of thought. There may also be a tendency toward hoarseness, dry coughs or head colds. They will find great joy and happiness in visiting or travelling through such places as Flanders, Egypt, India and most of all, the southern part of France.

Polarity A
25th August to 20th September

Those born in this polarity, between 25th August and 20th September, are generally shining lights in the educational and intellectual worlds. More women than men come into this period and become teachers of music, fine arts, or in a more humble way, creators of costumes or workers at fine sewing and other trades or arts requiring nimbleness of fingers and hands.

On the other hand, the men of this period have a natural tendency toward the spiritual things of life and would be excellent clergymen or teachers of ethics, philosophy and morals, if they could express themselves freely and outside of the limitations of sectarianism. People in this polarity are generally very genial, good-natured, polished, cultured and artistically and musically inclined. But this polarity also gives great strength of character and a dominating magnetism that would make them well qualified as physicians and surgeons, or judges and magistrates.

Children born in this polarity must be directed very carefully, because the imagination is highly developed, and this may create in them imaginary ideas that they will represent as truth and thereby fall into the habit of making false statements. They must also be guarded against a restlessness of nature, ever seeking the strange and peculiar things of life and ignoring the practical. Overstudy on the part of such children must be guarded against, because the nervous and mental systems will not stand the strain during childhood and early youth.

Polarity B
20th September to 15th October

Those born in this polarity, between 20th September and 15th October, are particularly well adapted to the use of their mental abilities and logical reasoning in making decisions and coming to reasonable conclusions. They are well balanced in all of their faculties and have a great desire to balance their thoughts and knowledge. In examining the evidence or the statements on any subject, or in any matter of dispute, they are sure to seek for the balance and to want to establish an equality in all things. The tendency in their lives is to be more or less aesthetic, with a great love for the pretty, beautiful, luxurious, nice and comfortable things of life.

They are generally supporters or patrons of the arts and music, as well as drama, and make good artists and writers, especially of happy and fantastic tales with good moral principles involved. They are seldom ruffled, seldom upset, and go through life with a tranquillity and evenness that is a great help to others as well as themselves. They should therefore occupy such positions as enable them to hold conditions in certain bounds, or to direct the lives of children and young people along the lines of peace, harmony and beauty.

Period No. 5
16th October to 6th December

Those born in this period, between 16th October and 6th December, generally attain great success and fame in their particular callings, although this success may not always be measured in worldly things or in a financial way. These people carry over from the past incarnation one lesson they have learned well and which becomes the keynote of their inner, secret natures and that is, that as one gives and does for others, so one attains and succeeds in life. Therefore, these people are fundamentally generous, good-natured, kindly and often free in their actions and lives to such an extent that their own success and progress seems to be nil from a material point of view, and for this reason they are often misjudged as failures in life.

On the other hand, they do acquire an unusual amount of knowledge, a great deal of culture and polish, an extreme amount of happiness and pleasure and are generally comfortable and satisfied with their lot in life, even though it may be in poor circumstances or in a humble position.

In every crisis, the cosmic comes to their rescue and brings about satisfactory conditions. This does not however prevent them from seeking greater things and a greater abundance of life's blessings. They are philosophically inclined through the lessons they have learned in the past and believe that they should give thanks every morning for life itself and not complain if they have the least of the worldly blessings. They realise they have in their knowledge and in their mystical powers a greater asset than most other human beings and for this they are eternally thankful. They also bring into this life from the cosmic, through the vibrations of the period in which they were born, an unusually philosophical nature, accompanied with the ability to acquire languages and to understand the spiritual and natural laws of the universe to an unusual degree. This makes it simple for them to acquire and master the principles of harmony in art, music, writing and even in chemistry.

Being capable therefore of expressing themselves in so many different ways, they are really in possession of more hobbies throughout life than those born in any other period. Whenever they seek relaxation or a change of occupation, they can turn their hands to music, mechanics, art or to the sciences, and dabble in any one of these things to a degree that almost borders upon professional expertness. For this reason they may enter into various occupations in their youth and change often as they go through life. They finally settle into positions where their complex abilities can be used, one by one, throughout the weeks and months and thereby hold unique positions that other people could not fill.

Fundamentally, there is a great love of animals, of outdoor sports, and of nature itself. They are open, frank, honest and cheerful, and deplore deceit and underhandedness. They have carried over with them a high degree of mystical development and of religious and spiritual attunement, and are often thrown into deep spells of spiritual meditation that others may view as despondency. They seem to sense the sufferings as well as the pleasures of the world.

These people would make excellent directors of organisations, where they are concerned with the scope of larger plans and things of a national or international importance rather than with the smaller details of executive management. They are capable of planning great schemes and carrying them out successfully, and for this reason they may enter the professions of advertisement writing and planning, sales organisation work, or the control and management of schools, colleges and universities. In business methods however, their generosity, charity and liberal nature does not bring them personal fortune, nor help to build up the financial end of their plans. But it does bring success in every other direction, which eventually leads to financial success. We are more apt to find such people in the positions of judges, senators, lawyers, priests, doctors of law, professors in universities, newspaper or magazine editors, shop keepers, antique dealers, or dealers in the arcane and mystical things of life.

Physically, the most common point of weakness is in connection with inflammation of various parts of the body, through colds accompanied by conditions of the blood due to overeating or irregular eating, or the eating of rich foods. Skin diseases, rheumatic conditions, quinsy and apoplexy are general conditions found with these people. They will find great joy and happiness in journeying through or visiting Babylon, Persia, Egypt, Palestine and the strange byways of the Orient where they may come in contact with ancient familiarities, especially in Egypt, China and Japan.

Polarity A
16th October to 11th November

Those born in this polarity, between 16th October and 11th November, are very aggressive in their business affairs because they have a nature that is filled with determination and energy, but do not rise to heights in the same channels as those in the B polarity. Those in the A polarity have a feeling that they must fight their way through life and must be everlastingly at something in order to keep themselves from slipping back into a mediocre position. The aggressiveness of the people in this polarity leads them into many unique positions and makes them outstanding characters in their ability to accomplish difficult things. They have a tendency however toward accidents and toward delays through their own rash exertions and these people will find themselves best fitted for positions in connection with government, or as attorneys, occupied daily in arguments and dissension, fighting for certain principles with considerable success.

Polarity B
11th November to 6th December

Those born in this polarity between 11th November and 6th December are almost the opposite of those born in the A polarity with regard to aggressiveness. The warlike spirit of their nature is greatly subdued and they would rather stay away from a quarrel or argument than take any part in it. They believe that everything will eventually adjust itself successfully and properly without contention. They are happier, more cheerful and free in their living than those in the A polarity and while not seeking positions, labours or problems that call for strenuous physical effort, they do love to tackle problems that call for mystical understanding or intellectual mastership and careful, logical reasoning for a solution.

These people make very dependable friends, are often leaders of humanitarian movements, and occupy themselves more in helping others than in helping themselves. They enjoy the nice things of life but always have an inclination to seek places that are covered, secret or out of the way, and associate with people who are of lowly or humble station and try to help them. On the other hand, they live an open and noble life, constantly trying to rise to the greatest of mystical heights and become spiritually attuned with the highest forces in the universe. Great masters, adepts and those ready for the highest forms of mystical initiation are generally found in this polarity.

Period No. 6
7th December to 27th January

Those born in this period bring with them from the past incarnation a benediction that they have earned through suffering and much trial and pain. This benediction is in the form of a reward and brings them happiness, joy and indulgence in the pleasant things of life which they have not had before, but which they may have had an opportunity to enjoy, but discarded or cast aside in some previous incarnation and then had to do without for a long time in order to learn a great lesson. However, being born in this period brings the benediction and blessing of attainment, peace and attunement with the pleasant, cheerful, lovely things of human life.

As they use these pleasures in this incarnation, so will they determine for themselves what their fate will be in the next. And if they abuse the benediction that is theirs this time or cast it lightly aside in any way, it will be denied to them at the close of this incarnation and in a future one. To carry out this benediction, the cosmic vibrations of this period have given them certain faculties and functions which, if developed and applied properly, will bring them the joy and happiness they deserve. They therefore have a natural tendency toward music, merriment, amusements, singing, a pleasant voice, pleasing disposition and a cheerful aspect of life.

There is a distaste born in them in this incarnation for anything sordid or deceitful, and virtue and honour are constant urges of their present inner dispositions. For this reason, they are not usually given to quarrelling or wrangling, or to viciousness of any kind. Early in childhood and throughout life they will show a tendency toward cleanliness in health, cleanliness in habits and even a conservative attitude toward all indulgences. This makes many of the people born in this period of the aesthetic type and we may easily recognise most of them by their physical appearance, for they seem to be of the mental temperament and what one would casually call the artistic or musical type.

They are seldom of very robust build or even of robust health. Naturally they tend to become musicians, artists, sculptors, actors, actresses, designers or teachers of these arts and professions. The men make excellent jewellers when they are not engaged in music, art or drama, or dealers in silks and fine dress materials, embroideries and things of this kind. While they may go into these lines of business for the money there is in them, the real instinctive reason is their desire to be with and around fine materials and artistic creations. For the same reason, they may go into the business of manufacturing and selling perfumes, or works of art and become engravers or dealers in commodities that are for personal adornment or the decoration of homes.

Such people need sympathetic understanding if one is to become well acquainted with them and they should never be forced to go into lines of business that deal with mechanics or heavy machinery, or coarse and muscular occupations. They are easily frightened and annoyed and should never be placed as children or young people where there is great disturbance and a lack of peace and quiet. For such people to be driven into war or into the melee of Wall Street or conditions of this kind is to be forced into an early annihilation of their best faculties and abilities, and to bring about a gradual breaking down of the body leading to early transition. They are really the makers of mirth in life and are usually the wholesome, sweet characters that we love to idealise.

In physical weaknesses, they generally suffer from nervousness, due to overstudy or unpleasant environment, or very often from the suppression of natural functions due to an extreme moral viewpoint. In fact, this moral viewpoint may lead some of them to refrain from marriage until late in life and in this repression they bring about a weakening of the constitution. Most of their physical suffering will be in parts of the body located in the abdomen and especially in the bladder, kidneys and bowels. They will find great joy and happiness in travelling through or visiting Arabia, parts of Austria, especially around Vienna, along the Mediterranean coast and England and the New England States of America.

Polarity A
7th December to 1st January

Those born in this polarity between 7th December and 1st January are a little more serious in life than those in Polarity B, for they generally have a tendency to want to teach and promulgate their aesthetic ideas and help establish these things in their own community or nation. For this reason they may become associated with reform movements, or with educational movements, promulgating philosophy and ethics. They often become critics of drama, art or music for it is their desire to separate the bad from the best in life and, even in all that seems perfect to others, they see flaws and can constructively and helpfully analyse and point out the errors that others do not see.

For this reason we find people in this polarity occupying very definite positions, generally as critics or teachers of a distinct class or even as judges in competitions, or as readers for magazines and newspapers where they may pass judgement upon matters that are submitted for use. Their analytical minds enable them to accomplish a great deal of good for humanity and especially in all the arts and sciences, where they are more successful as analytical experts than as real developers of any one of the principles involved in any of the sciences and arts.

Polarity B
1st January to 27th January

People born between 1st January and 27th January, are critical to an extreme extent and while they do not allow this criticism to be applied for the benefit of others (for they hesitate to become known as reformers or to be identified with the criticism of matters of any kind), they nevertheless become critical of their own lives and of their own actions. This causes them considerable unrest and often makes them of that type which we call *Aquarian*. In other words, they often find themselves changing their opinions and doing things hastily and impulsively because of a sudden impression or a sudden critical attitude. After the act is completed, or the words spoken, they again analyse and criticise their actions and wonder why they did or said the things that have passed.

These people also become antiquarians and love to delve into old bookshops, museums and places of research, for they find pleasure and happiness in analysing and criticising, examining and studying the unusual things of life. They make wonderful friends and are good entertainers, for they can talk well and long of unusual experiences and things they have witnessed or enjoyed in life. And there is the ability to build up stories and fictitious pictures and situations that enable them to become excellent writers of plays, dramas or scenarios.

They enjoy life in a peculiar way through indulgence in their own unique forms of pleasure, and are often looked upon as being Bohemian or unusual in life. They are never accused however of being peculiar in their mental equipment, or of being irrational in any sense. They are greatly loved by a large number of friends, and in parties, entertainment and associations, are far from being wallflowers or undesirable elements. They often attract to themselves an excellent companion for life in either marriage or business and are really one of the important types making up the complex nature of humanity.

Period No. 7
28th January to 21st March

Those born in this period, between 28th January and 21st March, carry from their previous lives into this one the necessity for accomplishing very serious and important work in connection with the evolution of humanity. They are those who have brought into their lives through their own actions in the last incarnation the need for learning: first the serious aspects of life and secondly, teaching these things to others through the example of their own living, or through their instruction.

They have usually gone through a great many incarnations and are highly evolved and experienced in the lessons to be learned from all the experiences that life has to give in many foreign lands. For this reason, early in life, these people as children or even as infants, would be called old souls and considered older than their years. From the cosmic they have also inherited as a gift the ability to recall much of their past instruction and most of the experiences they have had in life, along with the additional faculty of being able to formalise their knowledge. They readily acquire new knowledge and relate it to that which they have already stored up in the inner consciousness.

It is therefore not surprising to find that these people have an unusually deep imagination that seems to be prophetic and capable of imagining things that occurred in great antiquity, or that will occur in the future. They also have the ability to argue, to explain logically, and to present their thoughts and pictures systematically. They are reserved in their utterances and reserved and dignified in all of their actions. They give one the constant feeling of a person who feels that he or she is being observed, watched and analysed and must therefore be on guard in connection with every thought and act.

In judgement, they are severe because they are strict and careful. Unlike those in the fifth period, they do not allow their hearts to influence their judgements. To them, the law is the law and is both merciful and just, and no exceptions and variations of the law must be allowed because of sentiment. Therefore, being stern and just, they are generally greatly honoured and respected and seldom accused of being too severe or unfairly strict.

These people believe that the great things of life are attained through study and the careful building up of acquisitions along definite lines. They are extremely systematic, and take advantage of every principle of natural law and of man-made laws to assure themselves of the things they want in life and to protect what they have. They are not mercenary but on the other hand, they are not overly generous. They are, of course, naturally honest and more severe concerning the exactness of statement and precision of things than those in any of the other periods. For all these reasons, these people would make excellent judges, magistrates or heads of large corporations and big business propositions.

A peculiar thing is that in moderate circumstances and when born in mediocre positions, they often become employed in connection with such lines as plumbing, bricklaying, plastering, building, gardening, dyeing of cloth, printing, or in one of the other trades or businesses that are usually united in unions or under definite wage scales as labour trades. If these people only knew that their inherent desire for exactness, precision and truthfulness could lead them into higher occupations, such as magistrates and judges, they would seek education and training for such positions early in life and succeed well indeed.

On the other hand, their firm belief that the benefits and necessities of life can be acquired only by slow acquisition and the careful attainment of them, leads them into occupations that are well established, protected by union and government laws, and which seldom fluctuate in hours of employment or in salaries. They therefore hamper their own progress through a false understanding of the principles of life. Many of them also become nuns, monks or members of monastic organisations or bodies and live secluded lives where they can labour in their definite systematic manner to bring into their lives that which they feel is right.

Diseases that are natural to them through the vibrations of their period at birth, are impediments of the ears, teeth or eyes and sometimes of speech, and such conditions as proceed from colds, such as tuberculosis and often pneumonia. On the other hand, their excellent constitutions enable them to live to a very old age, and they suffer only from jaundice or dropsy, with occasionally a touch of palsy or apoplexy. These people are not usually ill until late in life and are able to fight off many of the ailments that come to others. They will find great joy and pleasure in visiting such countries as Turkey, the Balkans, Spain, parts of Africa and South America.

Polarity A
28th January to 23rd February

People born in this polarity, between 28th January and 23rd February, are often led into occupations that are unusual such as those of chemical experts, criminologists, investigators, explorers, research workers in ancient history, archaeology, geology and similar subjects. They are easily classified as being profound in knowledge and devoted to only one, or possibly two, subjects in life. They usually dress in a reserved manner and give the appearance of being much older than they are, with extreme reserve, a tendency toward orthodox and religious devotion, caring little for the gaieties of life and seldom patronising anything that is frivolous or transitory.

They are diligent workers, consistent, dependable, careful and often employed in the same positions or same lines of work throughout their entire lives. These people are often known as the salt of the earth and are wonderful friends to those who can make a contact beneath the surface and win their favour. There is a desire to reform the world in certain regards but they are consistent enough to adopt the reform themselves and live the life dictated by it, thereby setting an example.

Polarity B
23rd February to 21st March

Those born between 23rd February and 21st March, are quite opposite to those of Polarity A, as they are not quite so serious in life and do seek some pleasure and happiness as a relaxation and reaction from their more serious studies and occupations. The people in this polarity have an unusual tendency toward mysticism, occultism and the mysterious things of the universe and of nature. They also seem to acquire more fortune in a material sense than those in polarity A and often attain considerable fame in their particular fields of effort.

However, they are quite dual in nature and are capable of living a dual life inasmuch as they may be outwardly at the head of a great organisation, or contacting the public in a smiling, happy mood, while at home or in the privacy of their own seclusion, they may be quiet, reserved and more interested in the deeper, more serious things of life than one would suspect. They have a great magnetic power, which they can easily exert over others, and have a tendency to easily read the minds of other people and to project their consciousness into space and there sense the thoughts and actions of others. They also love to be near the water and enjoy taking long journeys, more for the purpose of studying human nature or studying the history and conditions of the country and place than for pleasure, although they do enjoy being on the water and in cities near it.

17 *Cycles of Reincarnation*

JUST AS EACH YEAR of our lives begins a new cycle and each one of these cycles is divided into periods of progression and development, with intermittent periods of action and reaction; and just as the general cycle of life is divided into periods of seven years through which we progress from a purely physical creature to a more or less perfected spiritual being, clothed in a physical body; so our whole existence in this universe is divided into larger periods of approximately 144 years which constitute the periods in a long cycle of incarnation and reincarnation.

Just as you who read this book today may be in the sixth period of your complex life cycle in this incarnation and in the fourth period of your yearly cycle, so you may be in the eighth, tenth, fiftieth or one hundredth period of your long cycle of reincarnations.

Whether or not one believes in the science of the evolution of species or not, there is one thing quite certain, and that is that the human being as a definite and distinct species, has been evolving steadily since the time it became a distinct creature with human traits. In other words, the thinking human being as a thinking man or woman, had a beginning, whether spontaneous, as the orthodoxy of some religions claim, or as the culmination of innumerable stages of evolution preceding its distinct human nature. Therefore, from the time of the emergence of the human being as the most evolved creature on earth, men and women have continued evolving, and this evolution will continue indefinitely.

We may liken the beginning of our career as a species to the production of a book. The critical materialist may say that a book with its beautiful binding, well printed pages, attractive illustrations, gold lettering and gilded edges, was nothing more or less at one time than a mass of cotton pulp, silkworm strands and mineral crystals. It may be truthfully said that the book we now admire evolved beautifully out of lesser things and therefore had a very primitive beginning in the elements of the earth, plant and animal life.

But the mystic or philosopher might reply and say that the book never was a book until all of these elements had been gathered together by a master mind, their natures changed, their tendencies altered, and new combinations created. In the twinkling of an eye they were brought together spontaneously into a new thing called a *book*, and preceding its creation as a book, it did not exist even in any primitive form.

The mystic therefore, is not concerned with what changes the evolution of earthly elements may have brought into the process of preparation for the physical composition of the human body. Mystics are concerned primarily with the creation of the person by the placing of the highest consciousness of God within a physical form and thereby spontaneously creating and bringing into existence a new species, a new creature, a new manifestation of Godliness.

From the time of the creation onward, the physical evolution that occurs in the body is purely secondary to the greater evolution that is occurring in a person's spiritual nature and soul-personality. It is unquestionably true that a person's physical form today is a vast improvement over the form that our primitive ancestors possessed. Unquestionably, the human physical form has evolved from a lower to a higher type, and such evolution has not reached its heights nor even sensed its ultimate goal. We are as responsible for this physical evolution as is God, for as we recreated our environment, it reacts upon both our physical and mental development and perfects the upward tendency of our evolution on earth.

The evolution of the human soul-personality proceeds through its contact with the experiences, trials, tribulations and lessons of this earthly life, as well as through its contact with the universal Divine consciousness of the cosmic Mind of God. Mystics and devout students of religion of all lands realise that the spiritual evolution and perfection of the human being could not occur in the short period of one incarnation. That would be equivalent to but one period of seven years in the earthly life cycle of each person here on earth. If we look upon the earthly life cycle and realise that each seven years brings its progress and increasing evolution to the soul-personality and mind, as well as to the body of each individual on this earth plane, we will realise how different it would be if each of us lived but one period of that cycle for instance, from our birthday to our seventh year.

Certain wonderful changes and improvements in the body, mind and soul-personality would unquestionably take place in that short span of existence. But look at the remarkable changes that occur in the next period, from the seventh to the fourteenth birthday and then again from the fourteenth to the twenty-first and so on.

If we think of the evolution and cycle of the soul-personality and of the existence here on earth in a physical body as being like the periods of a life cycle, we will see that each incarnation in a physical body is like a period of seven years in the earthly cycle. It is only through progressive experiences and the continuation of those and other experiences that we can evolve. If there were but one period in which we lived on earth and if that period were even three, four or five hundred years long, it would not be sufficient for each soul-personality to learn all that it must learn, to suffer all that it must suffer, to master all that it must master, and attain all that is attainable in order to reach that degree of perfection that would constitute a reason for our existence at all.

How often we notice a young man or woman of brilliant mind and of unusual capabilities and ask the question, how old is he, or how old is she? We want to know whether these young people are in the second or third period of their earthly life cycle. In other words, we want to know whether they are in the period between seven and fourteen, or fourteen and twenty-one. This is to enable us to comprehend the reason for the extraordinary mental development or spiritual progress we notice them. Is it not just as appropriate then, when we find a person highly evolved in spiritual things, well developed in the mastership over earthly conditions and greatly illumined in the mystical and natural laws of the universe, to ask in what incarnation is this person?

We are really asking whether the person is in the third, fourth, twentieth, fiftieth or one hundredth period of incarnation on the earth plane. Of course we have no way of answering such questions but still we ask them and wonder about it. We often notice in young people that look, that poise, that character, that something that warrants us saying: *"This is an old soul."* Where does this universal feeling that some have lived much longer than others come from?

This is not a plea on behalf of the doctrine of reincarnation, for the doctrine itself needs no plea at my hands, and this is not the place in which to present an outline of the doctrine, or submit any of a thousand or more arguments to substantiate it. My sole intention here is to arouse questions in your mind and start some very interesting thinking that may lead you to some worthwhile conclusions.

A few years ago the mere mention of any idea connected with the belief in reincarnation elicited smiles and facetious comments. Today, clergymen of many denominations and leaders in their respective fields of work, eminent writers, philosophers, editors, physicians and scientists freely comment on their belief in reincarnation. They point out that it is the only merciful, just, logical, sane and rational explanation of the differences we see in life and of the inequalities, the tests, trials, joys and blessings enjoyed so differently by all human beings.

The doctrine was once a fundamental principle of the Christian religion but was arbitrarily rejected by those who could not comprehend it, and today Christianity is one of the few in which the doctrine is completely set aside and misunderstood. Fortunately, some great leaders in the Christian church are reviving the doctrine again through a gradual comprehension of its real principles and of its truth.

The important point I wish to impress upon your mind is that the doctrine of reincarnation presents to us the one dominating and overtone cycle of life by which all other cycles are standardised and from which all other undulating periods emanate. Without a comprehension of the cycle of incarnations, all other cycles are incomprehensible, and one may say that without a comprehension of the true nature of our ontological existence, all other details of our earthly life or of our spiritual existence in the universe are similarly incomprehensible.

Let those who read this book therefore, find it within their hearts or within the scope of their rational thinking to lay aside bias and prejudice and look into the greater truths that are offered by the mystic and student of true spiritual laws. Read such books as will give you a better understanding of your true relationship to the universe, to God and to humanity. Discover your own place in the life you are living and in the lives of all other beings. Learn the powers that you possess and thereby break through the fictitious wall of limitations that has been placed about you by human man creeds and modern doctrines. Expand your consciousness until you become attuned with the infinite, where all truths, all laws and all principles will appeal to the rationalism of your soul and the wisdom of the Divine Mind within you. This will bring added degrees of mastership and leadership. Within you and about your own existence are the greatest fields for exploration that humanity has ever known.

And while you are delving into the mysteries of your business, your social, financial and other affairs, do not neglect to delve into the mysteries of your life, the mysteries of your own being. In other words, recall the ancient scriptural injunction: *"With all thy getting, get understanding."*

REFERENCE INDICATOR

This book postulates that in life, there are so-called 'fortunate' and 'unfortunate' periods for every type of activity we wish to engage in, and we are free to cooperate with or go against the general flow of universal influences at any given time. It is all a question of how much effort we wish to expend in doing a particular thing through choosing a 'good' or 'bad' period in which to do it. To assist you in determining when you enter and leave any of the seven periods within the 24 hour day, we have created a small reference indicator that will remind you, at a glance, which period you are in.

This handy reference indicator can be carried in your pocket and is ever ready to reveal the tendencies of the cycles affecting you. Accompanying it is a leaflet that fully explains the things to avoid during certain periods, or the profitable periods that await you. Using this indicator often will soon ensure that you commit to memory all seven periods for the seven days of the week. If you do not already have one, you can order the reference indicator and leaflet today from:-

The Rosicrucian Collection	Tel:	+44-(0)1892-653197
Greenwood Gate, Blackhill	Fax:	+44-(0)1892-667432
Crowborough TN6 1XE	email:	sales@amorc.org.uk
United Kingdom	Website:	ww.amorc.org.uk

The reference indicator below resembles
a large coin made from a brass alloy.

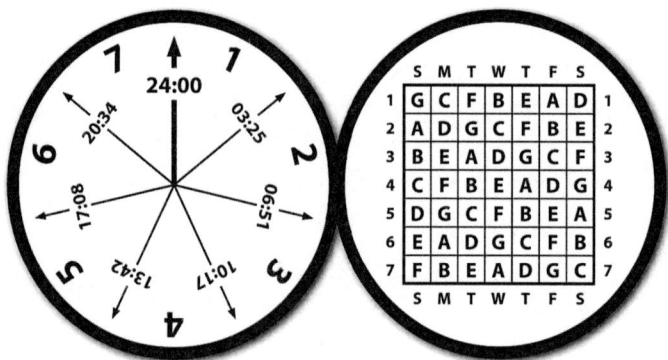

	S	M	T	W	T	F	S	
1	G	C	F	B	E	A	D	1
2	A	D	G	C	F	B	E	2
3	B	E	A	D	G	C	F	3
4	C	F	B	E	A	D	G	4
5	D	G	C	F	B	E	A	5
6	E	A	D	G	C	F	B	6
7	F	B	E	A	D	G	C	7
	S	M	T	W	T	F	S	

FRONT   BACK

THE ROSICRUCIAN ORDER®

SOME REFERENCES were made in this book to the Rosicrucian Order.[1] Therefore, anticipating questions you may have, we would like to take this opportunity to explain the purpose of the Rosicrucian Order and how you may learn more about it.

The Rosicrucian Order uses modern educational tools to bring out the highest qualities of creativity, human goodness and sanctity in all who seek a comprehensive way of living that will bring them closer to their ideal of a life lived in harmony with nature and the spiritual laws governing human life. For those who seek a deeper meaning and transcendent purpose to life, the Order teaches highly effective techniques to enable people to experience their innate spirituality in the broadest, most tolerant and universal manner possible. The pursuit of spiritual experience, awareness and mystical wisdom is regarded by many as the most important of all human endeavours. Those who have the courage, patience and fortitude to seek it out, regardless of the challenges involved, will find within this Order of mystics, a warm and loving spiritual home.

---

1   Some organisations have in their titles words such as *Rosicrucian, Rose-Cross, Rosy-Cross, Rozenkreuz* or words similar to them, but those organisations have no links with the true Rosicrucian Order. There is only one universal Rosicrucian Order® in the world today, united in 19 language jurisdictions under the direction of a single governing body, the *Supreme Grand Lodge of the Ancient and Mystical Order Rosae Crucis.*

Although encouraging a deep sense of spirituality in the broadest, most universal sense possible, the Rosicrucian Order is not a religion. It is not sectarian, imposes no prescribed dogma, and instructs people from widely diverse social, educational, political and religious strata in 17 different languages in virtually every country in the world. The Order retains in modern form the ancient landmarks, traditions and practical helpfulness of the original Rosicrucian fraternity as founded centuries ago. It is known throughout the world as the *Ancient and Mystical Order Rosae Crucis* (often abbreviated as AMORC). The publishers of this book, *The Rosicrucian Collection*®, is a wholly owned subsidiary of the English Grand Lodge of the Rosicrucian Order for Europe, the Middle East and Africa, located at...

Greenwood Gate,
Blackhill,
Crowborough.
TN6 1XE
United Kingdom

Tel: +44-(0)1892-653197
Fax: +44-(0)1892-667432
Email: sales@amorc.org.uk

If you wish to know more about the Rosicrucian Order, please continue reading, or visit our international website at *www. amorc.org* and choose your language and region preference.

Rosicrucians and Mysticism

THE ROSICRUCIAN ORDER uses the word "mystical" in its official title, and for good reason; for the disciplines associated with mysticism have always been the surest and most accurate method of personal spiritual discovery.

When correctly applied to daily situations, the various disciplines associated with the "mystical quest" opens one to insights into several areas of research currently beyond the realm of scientific enquiry. Mysticism has the potential of leading sincere seekers of esoteric knowledge not only to deeper insights into many of the remaining unknowns of science, but more importantly, can lead them to states of personal accomplishment, happiness and peace beyond their greatest expectations.

Mysticism is however not merely a matter of gaining intellectual knowledge, for there are many excellent colleges and universities that serve the human intellect best in that area. Mysticism requires no arduous academic training, no formulas, names or dates to learn by rote; and there are no exams other than those that life itself compels one to pass. Mysticism does however require sincerity of purpose and dedicated work on the improvement of one's self towards a personally acknowledged higher ideal.

In one respect, the discipline of mysticism attempts to establish a conscious link between oneself and a certain source of knowledge that presently lies beyond the limits of science. In another respect, and one that has been spoken of eloquently within widely diverse religious and philosophical systems over thousands of years, mysticism seeks to unite the life experience of the individual with what each of those religions and philosophies experienced as a supreme, over-arching reality often referred to simply as "God."

That a source of wisdom and inspiration of this nature has an independent existence beyond the scope of normal human intellect, has been attested to by many of the greatest minds of the past and continues to be eloquently spoken of by some of the greatest thinkers of our own era. And this source of wisdom, in a nutshell, is what mysticism seeks to bring into a living reality in the life of every sincere person who seeks it.

Through a study and application of the principles taught by the Rosicrucian Order, one can learn to recognise and respond to a source of infallible wisdom that already exists within oneself. With sharpness and focused purpose, the advice one receives seems to originate from the very depths of one's own being. What could be more satisfying than discovering in one's own time, at one's own pace and on one's own initiative, new and exciting truths that have immediate and practical use in one's life?

This inner guidance has variously been called the *"still, small voice within,"* the *"Inner Self,"* or the *"Master Within."* In most cultures there is a name for it, for in every human being there is a recognisable deeper nature or personality of immense potential, a nature of considerable sophistication, refinement and capacity for development that merely needs to be found and brought to the surface or awareness.

Every human being, without exception, has this embryonic potential just waiting to be released. Your "inner sanctity" plays its part constantly in guiding and urging you to do what you know to be right for yourself, for your loved ones, and even for those you care very little about but must nevertheless interact with daily.

In developing your awareness of this inner life, you soon learn of the inherent error of relying *exclusively* on your objective senses and thought processes when coming to important decisions. There is a different, more refined, sophisticated and accurate method of getting *precisely* the answers you want, and the Rosicrucian Order assists people through its system of instruction, how to accomplish this.

On a purely practical level, the study and application of mystical techniques leads to the development of a more mature and integrated personality, greater success in your daily activities, and a growing feeling of happiness and peace in your personal affairs. Although the benefits of being a Rosicrucian are also of a deeper and more transcendental nature, if peace and happiness were the only things that entered your life in abundance, would it not still be worth your while pursuing such a path?

The Rosicrucian techniques of self-development include specific and highly effective methods of concentration, visualisation, contemplation and meditation, to mention but a few; and a proper study and application of these techniques can provide you with exceedingly powerful tools to help you shape your life at all levels, whether physical, mental, psychic or spiritual.

If you are seeking a new path in life, or simply wish to know more about your options, you are invited to investigate further by contacting us and requesting the free introductory booklet entitled *The Mastery of Life*. In it you learn who we are, where we come from and what you can gain by allowing the Rosicrucian Order to assist you in creating your own customised path of inner development.